The Healthy Garden

The Healthy Garden

How to Control Pests, Diseases and Weeds

Edited by Kenneth A Beckett

Orbis · London

Acknowledgments

Photographs were supplied by A-Z Botanical Collection, B Alfieri, Alphabet and Image, Heather Anger, Barnaby's Picture Library, Pat Brindley, Brinsley Burbridge/Nature Photographers, S Buczacki, NA Callow, NA Callow/NHPA, GJ Cambridge/NHPA, Michael Chinery, John Clegg, Bruce Coleman/Bruce Coleman Ltd, RJ Corbin, John KB Cowley, Eric Crichton/Bruce Coleman Ltd, E Crowson, Philip Damp, Adrian Davies, Dickinson/Lucas, East Malling Research Station, Valerie Finnis, Vaughan Fleming, R Fletcher/Bob Gibbons Photography, R Fotheringham/NHPA, Brian Furner, Bob Gibbons, Glasshouse Crops Research Institute, F Greenaway/NHPA, J Hamilton, Iris Harwick Library, Brian Hawkes, George Hyde, ICI, Archivio IGDA, Martin King and Mike Reid, J Markham, John Mason, Tania Midgely, Richard Mills, Murphy Chemical Ltd, Walter Murray/NHPA, National Vegetable Research Station, Nature Photographers, Oxford Scientific Films, Premaphotos Wildlife, KG Preston-Mafham/NHPA, KG Preston-Mafham/Premaphotos Wildlife, Ray and Baker, Shell International Petroleum Co Ltd, D Smith, Harry Smith Horticultural Photographic Collection, A South, Sudburys, Pamela Toler, MWF Tweedie, S Viola, Michael Warren, Weed Research Organisation, D Wildbridge, MC Wilkes/Aquila Photographics, P Wilson.

Some of this material has previously appeared in *Green Fingers*

First published in Great Britain by
Orbis Publishing Limited, London, 1984

ISBN 0-85613-587-9

Printed in Italy

CONTENTS

INTRODUCTION

Many gardeners tend to think of pests, diseases and weeds as something peculiar to their gardens. True, particular problems can be greater in some gardens than in others, but enemies are present wherever plants exist and are an inescapable fact of life. The observant gardener will soon see examples of plants under attack in even the wildest countryside.

If a plant is not doing well, the answer is not to spray it with every pesticide and fungicide on the market. This may indeed harm it, especially if all that is wrong is that the plant needs moving from sun to shade or vice versa. The important thing is to try to identify what the problem is. Learn to recognise which part or parts of the plant are affected – leaves, flowers, roots, stem, trunk etc. Look up the plant in the appropriate A-Z section in the book, check out the pests and diseases referred to in the entry to see which produce these symptoms, and treat accordingly.

Having acknowledged the presence of pests, diseases and weeds, it is reassuring to know that they don't have to be a major worry. If your plants are healthy and vigorous, they are much less likely to suffer severe attacks from insects and fungi, and more able to resist them if they do. Given a good start in life most plants will thrive.

CREATING A HEALTHY GARDEN

Assuming that your plants are in a healthy condition to begin with, (and it is worth ordering them from a good nursery to achieve this) the important thing is to ensure that growing conditions are the best you can provide.

Soil analysis
One of the most important tasks is to maintain the correct balance of acidity or alkalinity according to the plants being grown. Some subjects grow better in an alkaline (limey or chalky) soil while others, such as rhododendrons, will grow only in an acid one (free of lime or chalk). The majority of garden plants, however, much prefer a soil that is midway between these two extremes.

Before you prepare your soil for planting it is advisable to carry out a soil test with one of the soil-testing kits that are available from garden centres and good department stores. Such a test will indicate the degree or intensity of acidity or alkalinity. This is measured on a logarithmic scale called the pH scale. On this scale pH 7 is neutral (neither acid nor alkaline) while lower numbers indicate increasing degrees of acidity and higher numbers show increasing degrees of alkalinity. A wide range of commonly-grown plants, including vegetables, fruit, roses, hardy perennials, trees and shrubs, grow best in a slightly acid to neutral soil of pH 6·5–7·0.

High acidity or alkalinity If your soil pH is below 5·5 then many plants may fail to grow and the numbers of undesirable organisms increase rapidly.

On the other hand an excessively limey soil, with a pH of over 8·0, can produce many plant disorders. Certain important plant foods, particularly iron and magnesium (but also manganese), are made unavailable to plants if the soil is limey. If a plant cannot absorb sufficient iron then its leaves will turn yellow and it may become stunted and eventually die. This yellowing is known as lime-induced

Soil-testing kits are readily available.

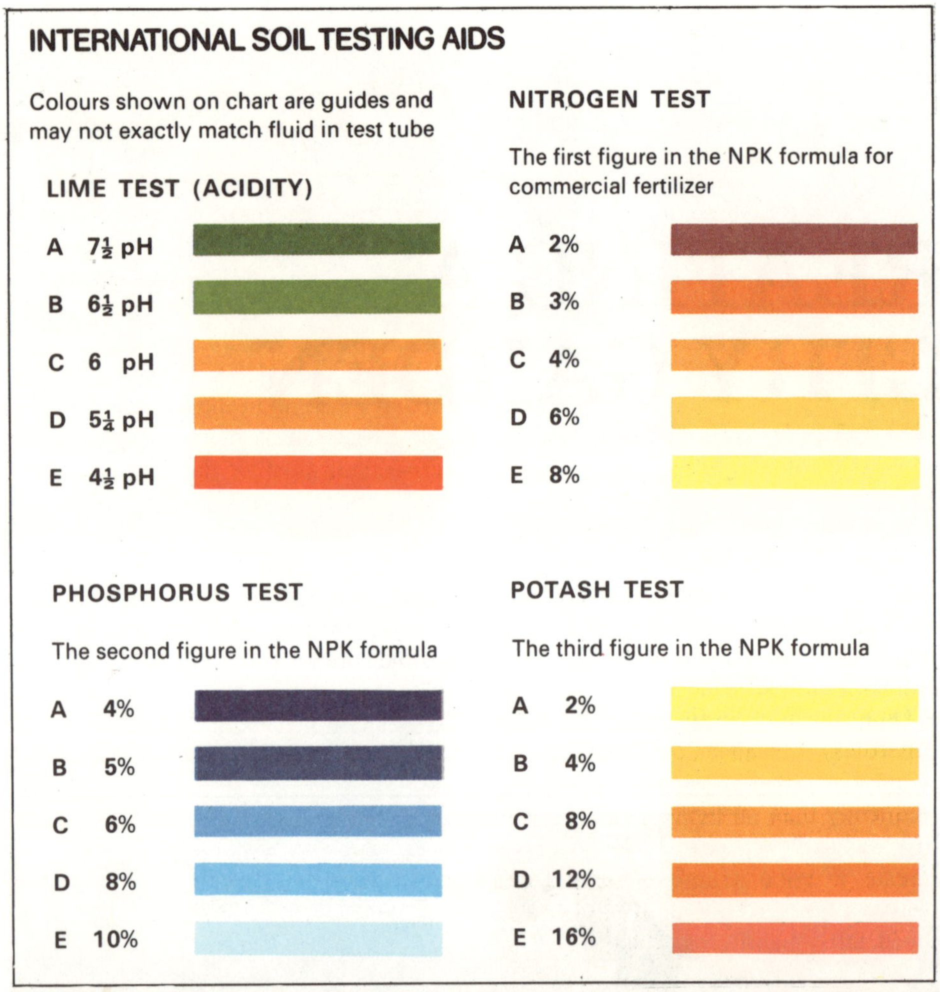

chlorosis. Bushes (particularly fruit bushes, roses and hydrangeas) and fruit trees quickly show symptoms of chlorosis if iron is not available. You can, however, cure this condition with annual drenches of a solution of sequestrene (applied according to maker's instructions); this supplies iron in a readily-available form.

How to make a soil test When using the soil-testing kit, quarter-fill the test tube (supplied with the kit) with soil and add the lime test solution, following the instructions provided. Then shake the tube to mix the contents thoroughly. Allow the solution to settle. When the soil has settled the clear liquid above will be of a certain colour according to the acidity or alkalinity of the soil. This colour can vary from red (when the soil is very acid) through orange (when only slightly acid) to shades of green (when the soil is neutral or limey). A chart showing the various colours with the appropriate pH number alongside is included in the kit. The liquid in the tube

Left: soil-testing kits can check a range of chemical balances in your soil. Below: mauve hydrangeas reflect a neutral pH level in the soil.

Above: clay soils can be opened up by the application of a top dressing of hydrated lime after digging.

must be matched with one of these colours in order to ascertain the pH of your soil.

Gardening on alkaline soil Some plants like a reasonably limey soil (pH of up to 8·0). Examples of these are members of the cabbage family (including wallflowers and aubrietia), carnations and pinks, beech, hornbeam, box, yew, clematis, gypsophila, and scabious. Cabbages and wallflowers suffer far less from club root disease (that causes the roots to swell and the plants to become stunted) if grown in a limey soil. Another interesting fact is that hydrangeas produce blue flowers in an acid soil, but pink blooms in alkaline conditions. If the soil is neutral, the blooms will be mauvish.

To lower the pH of a soil (reduce its alkalinity) you can incorporate heavy dressings of peat, leaf mould, well-rotted manure or garden compost each year. Applying flowers of sulphur will also reduce the pH but a heavy application is needed to reduce the pH by even one unit. For example, to reduce it from 8·0 to 7·0 would necessitate a dressing of about 1kg per sq m (2 lb per sq yd).

In chalky or limey areas it is probably inadvisable to use tap water for pot plants as the water will be alkaline and could result in chlorosis. Instead try to use rainwater or the water obtained from defrosting the fridge or freezer, as this will be 'soft' or acid.

Acid soils To raise the lime content of an acid soil, treat it with a dressing of hydrated lime or ground chalk. Usually this application is made in the winter after you have finished digging over the garden. Allow the lime to lie on the surface over the winter and then fork it in in the spring. Do not apply manure and lime at the same time.

On heavy or clay soils apply lime more generously – as much as 500g per sq m (1 lb per sq yd) at one time – but less frequently than on light or sandy types; lime helps to open up and flocculate (create a good crumb structure) the heavier type of soil. Sandy soils are best limed fairly lightly, 135–270g per sq m (4–8 oz per sq yd) annually. On such soils lime is easily leached, or washed out, by heavy rain. Sandy soils are generally more acid than clay soils and peaty soils are often excessively acid.

If the soil is very acid, say a pH of 5.0 or below, it is inadvisable to apply a large quantity of lime in a single application in order to bring the pH value up to slight acidity or neutral. Instead, apply a moderate dressing – about 500g per sq m (1 lb per sq yd) – regularly each winter.

How to improve difficult soils
For all except lovers of wet conditions, a soil that is well drained but not dry and is well laced with organic matter is ideal.

Soils can be divided into four main types: clays, sands, chalk soils and loams. Loams come midway between clays and sands. They are usually easy to work and provide ideal conditions for plants. Clay, sand and chalk each have special characteristics that can make them difficult soils and it may take several years to turn them into easily-managed growing mediums.

Clay Clay is commonly known as a heavy soil because it is very hard to cultivate – both to dig and to prepare for seed sowing or planting in the spring. Because of its chemical composition it has a very dense, or close, structure. It is able to hold large amounts of water within the clay particles, causing them to swell. Water is also held on the surface of the particles, and the particles themselves are held together by electrostatic attraction. It is therefore a very wet and sticky soil and takes a long time to dry out and warm up in the spring.

During the autumn and winter, and in wet weather at other times of year, clay may become waterlogged and this will adversely affect the health of plants growing in it. When a soil is holding too much water the oxygen supply to plant roots is reduced and if this condition continues over too long a period the plants may die.

On the other hand, in hot weather during spring and summer clay soils can become as hard as rock; for as they dry out the clay particles contract, making cultivation almost impossible.

OPENING UP CLAY SOILS Dig clay soils, ideally, in early to mid winter (November to December) so that frosts can break them down throughout the winter. Frosts will make a heavy soil more crumbly and therefore far easier to cultivate in the spring. You can also make a clay soil more crumbly, and take out most of the stickiness, by applying a top dressing of horticultural gypsum (sulphate of lime) immediately after digging (unless you have incorporated manure or compost as well). Leave it on the surface and it will be washed in by rain. Gypsum can generally be obtained from good gardening shops and centres. Apply it fairly generously each year, at a rate of 500g–1kg per sq m (1–2 lb per sq yd).

Hydrated lime has a similar effect to gypsum. Again it can be applied as a top dressing after digging. Apply it as evenly as possible. An application every two or three years is adequate for most crops.

It is interesting to note that, though gypsum improves the soil without raising the pH level (increasing alkalinity), hydrated lime raises the pH as well. Both cause flocculation (create a good crumb structure), thus improving the soil texture, drainage and aeration.

During the actual digging, incorporate

A SUMMARY OF SOIL TYPES

TYPES	PROBLEMS	ADVANTAGES	HOW TO IMPROVE
CLAY Smooth, not gritty, often wet, sticky and slimy in winter and brick-like in summer	The very small particles stick together when wet, making a solid, almost airless mass. Heavy and difficult to dig and break down. Cold – takes a long time to warm up in spring. Dries out slowly, unevenly and in clods. Seeds germinate poorly (because of lack of air) and plant roots have difficulty in growing (because it is so heavy and solid).	Usually rich in plant food. Can hold water well in dry summers. Is receptive to the addition of plant and animal organic matter, which will decompose by physical, chemical and bacterial activity in the soil. This completely decomposed material is called humus, which is rich in plant foods, gives the soil 'body' and encourages the retention of food, water and air. In particular, it helps to make clay more workable by breaking down the mass.	Unless already alkaline (chalky), spread garden lime – 375g per sq m (12 oz per sq yd) – all over dug soil in autumn and let the weather work it in. Otherwise fork in during to dig and cultivate. For lasting improvement dig in large quantities of organic (animal and plant) matter in early spring for several years. This will rot down in the soil, gradually improving structure and colour. Preferably use 'strawy' farmyard manure, otherwise plenty of peat and garden compost. Continue organic treatment every year, liming every 2–3 years. Do not mix lime with other fertilizers; apply 1 month before, or 2–3 months after, other soil conditioners. If clay is very heavy, artificial drainage may be required.
SAND Light and dry, gritty, crumbly and rough to handle	Poor in plant food. Unable to retain moisture; rainwater passes right through, leaching (washing out) plant foods into the subsoil out of reach of plant roots. Can be very acid due to leaching of lime.	Easy to work at any time of year. Warms up quickly after winter so cultivation can begin early in spring. Plenty of air in soil, allowing plant roots to grow strongly and deeply. Excellent for vegetables, especially root crops, when sufficient organic matter is added to retain water.	Manure, peat and compost must be dug in deeply to increase the soil's organic content. This will add plant foods and increase food- and moisture-retaining abilities. Treatment must be repeated yearly Also add general fertilizer before sowing or planting in spring and autumn. A light sprinkling of lime should be added every other year if soil is acid. Watering with nitrogenous fertilizer is advantageous throughout the growing season. Artificial watering will probably be necessary during dry spring and summer periods.
CHALK OR LIMESTONE Variable, often shallow, topsoil with recognizable lumps of chalk or limestone, especially in lower soil	Lacks humus and plant food. Difficult to work when wet. Tends to dry out quickly in summer. The calcium in chalk or limestone soil inhibits plants from using many plant foods, and deficiencies may result. Chalky soil is alkaline, and not tolerated by most plants.	Generally light, easy to work, free-draining and warms up quickly in spring. Good for rock garden plants.	Add large quantities of farmyard manure, compost or other organic matter, preferably to the top layer of soil, each spring and autumn. This will break down (into humus) in the soil, improving its condition. Give top dressings of general fertilizers throughout the growing season.
PEAT Dark brown or black, spongy to touch	Usually waterlogged and may need artificial drainage. May be very acid and sour. Often deficient in plant foods.	Contains plenty of organic matter as it consists mainly of organic material not yet fully decomposed. Easily worked. Too acid for most garden plants but very fertile when drained and limed.	If soil is waterlogged, then a soakaway or drainage pipes may be needed. Liming helps drainage and counteracts acidity. Add lime at 250g per sq m (8 oz per sq yd) every 2–3 years. Add regular, fairly heavy, dressings of general-purpose fertilizers in spring, summer and autumn.
LOAM Dark, crumbly, easy to clean from fingers	Should not be any problem as long as the drainage is satisfactory and the humus and plant food content is maintained.	Ideal garden soil, with a balanced mixture of sand, humus and clay. If humus content is maintained, a well-drained, well-aerated soil, rich in plant food, will result. Warm enough for early cultivation.	The improvements depend on the proportions of clay and sand in the loam. Sandy loam will require the regular spring and autumn addition of organic matter and fertilizers. Clayey loam may need regular addition of 375g per sq m (12 oz per sq yd) every 2–3 years. Heavy loams will benefit from being roughly dug over in autumn.

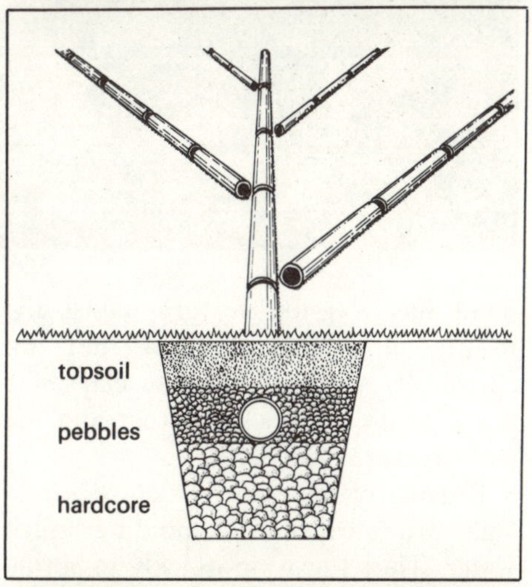

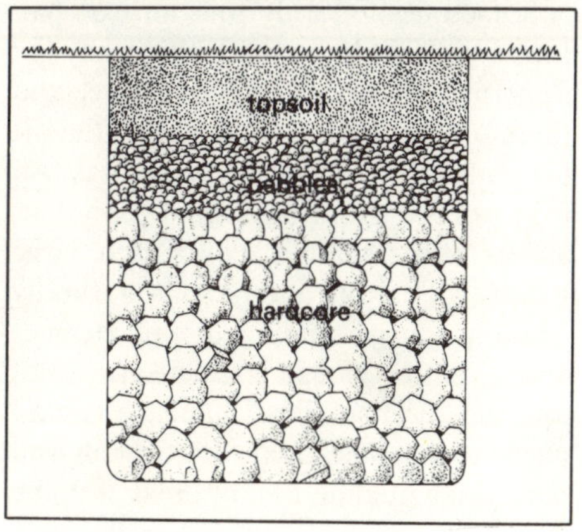

as much organic matter as possible to 'open up' the soil and to prevent it forming into large clods. This should give better drainage of surplus water and improve aeration. There are various types of organic matter that are suitable, such as well-rotted farmyard or horse manure, garden compost, peat, leaf mould, spent hops, bracken, straw, composted seaweed and composted sawdust. Try to apply at least one barrowload per square metre or yard. It is best to double dig clay soil as this will enable you to get the organic matter down into the lower soil. When double digging, keep the soil in its proper layers: never mix topsoil with subsoil.

Do not apply lime and manure at the same time, but try to leave an interval of at least two months between applications. Dig in organic material in the autumn, and scatter lime in early spring.

Spring is also the time to apply a general-purpose fertilizer prior to sowing and planting. It is not much use applying this in the autumn or winter, as most of the plant foods will have been washed too far down in the soil to be of any use.

Above: the compost heap provides good organic manure at little cost.
Right top: laying clay pipes for drainage.
Right centre: cross section of herringbone drainage system. Lower centre: upside-down turfs form top layer of soakaway.
Bottom: cross section of a soakaway.

DRAINAGE FOR CLAY SOILS If your garden soil is constantly waterlogged in wet weather, and none of the other cultural recommendations prove successful, it may be advisable to install a drainage system. However, this can be a costly operation and may prove difficult in a small garden.

Basically it involves laying a system of earthenware land drainpipes in the lower soil in a herringbone pattern. The main central pipe, that takes the water from the lateral pipes, should slope gently to a soakaway or ditch at the lowest point of the site. The lateral pipes slope gently to the main pipe.

Sand Sandy soils are the opposite of clays. They are generally known as 'light' soils because they are easy to work with.

Above: peat, though expensive, is an excellent mulch for sandy gardens. Left: well rotted stable manure can also help to improve the soil. Below: dug-out trench reveals 'tired' topsoil and subsoil that needs improving with humus.

Sand has a gritty texture, consisting mostly of grains of silica that are chemically stable. So, unlike clays, the particles do not stick together and the soil structure is loose.

Because of this loose structure, sandy soils are incapable of holding much water. They warm up quickly in spring but during dry weather they can dry out very rapidly and cause plants to wilt or die through lack of moisture. Again, because of their loose structure and chemical stability, sandy soils cannot hold much plant food and so are called 'hungry'.

FEEDING SANDY SOILS It is not necessary to dig sandy soils as early as heavy clay types, but even so digging should still be completed well before it is time to sow and plant in the spring. Ordinary single digging to the depth of a spade should be sufficient.

Sometimes in sandy soils an iron pan forms in the lower soil that may be impermeable to air and moisture, and therefore harmful to plants in that it prevents surplus water draining away. An iron pan is a rock-hard layer of soil that, as the name implies, contains a large quantity of iron. Sandy soils naturally contain a large amount of this element and, over the years, it is leached (by rain) into the lower soil where it cements sand particles together. If you discover an iron pan, you would do best to break it up by double digging the site. Thereafter you can single dig as it will probably be many years before a pan forms again.

The main consideration in improving sandy soils is to incorporate as much organic matter as possible to supply humus. Most sandy soils are seriously lacking in humus and so have a very poor structure, the soil being unable to hold water and plant foods. The humus acts as

a sponge and ensures adequate moisture for your plants during dry periods. Apply plenty of organic matter every year (provided this ties in with the cropping programme) for it quickly disappears in this type of soil. Also apply a general-purpose fertilizer in spring.

Chalk In some respects chalk soils are similar to sands. If you have only a thin layer of soil overlying chalk you will often be faced with lack of moisture during dry weather due to the percolation of water down through the chalk out of reach of plant roots. Such a soil will also be lacking in humus and plant foods. An additional problem with chalk soils is high alkalinity that can cause many plants to show symptoms of chlorosis (dwarfing of the plant and yellowing of the leaves). This occurs because the plants are not obtaining sufficient iron from the soil; iron becomes unavailable to plants when they are growing in conditions of high alkalinity. Roses, many soft and top fruits, hydrangeas and ericaceous plants (such as rhododendrons, azaleas and heathers) are prone to chlorosis.

Soils over limestone should be treated as chalk soils; it is often forgotten that chalk is a pure form of limestone.

IMPROVING CHALK SOILS Chalk soils (especially thin soils overlying solid chalk) need plentiful additions of organic matter; on some types it is almost impossible to apply too much. On such a site you would do best to dig as deeply as possible each year – preferably double digging. This will enable you to get organic matter well down into the soil so that, over a number of years, you gradually increase the depth of suitable growing soil. Also add organic matter to the topsoil – mix it well in if possible. Any of the kinds of organic matter suggested for clay soils can be used, but very acid materials (such as peat and leaf moulds) are particularly suitable as they help to reduce alkalinity – if only very slightly.

Alkalinity can be reduced by incorporating flowers of sulphur into the soil, but very large applications are necessary to do any good; you would need to use about 500g–1kg per sq m (1–2 lb per sq yd) every year.

With chalk as with sand, apply a general-purpose fertilizer in spring before you begin to sow or plant rather than in autumn or winter.

Above: mulching trees and shrubs with compost will conserve the moisture and help reduce the growth of weeds.
Below: a well balanced soil will provide an excellent crop of vegetables.

TUDOR
PRESSURISED
INSECTICIDE
SPRAYER

PESTS, DISEASES AND DISORDERS

Pests are a sub-class of animals that need plants for food. When their feeding habits conflict with human interests they become pests. Damage ranges from the total grazing of deer, rabbits or escaped farm stock, to the nibblings, funnellings and suckings of specialized insects that may confine their attentions to flowers (blossom weevil), fruit (codling moth), leaves (the larvae – caterpillars, of many sorts of butterfly and moth), stems (leopard moth and tunnelling beetle larvae), and roots (swift moth and chafer grubs). In addition there is the sap-sucking of aphids, capsid bugs etc, that results in stunting and malformation. Gardeners must be continually on the lookout for signs of damage, identifying the culprits and taking remedial action as soon as possible.

Pests will attack most plants, whether they live in the garden, the house or the greenhouse. As with illnesses and disorders, prevention is better than cure and the best way to reduce your losses is to ensure that your plants are healthy when planted and then well cared for. Many physiological disorders of plants (caused, for instance, by too little water or too much nitrogen fertilizer) pave the way for attack by pests. So as soon as you notice any signs of distress or damage—act promptly.

Knowing what to look for
The pest itself may be almost invisible. Eelworms, for instance, are difficult to see under a microscope. But their size bears no relation to the damage they can do. Even visible pests may not always be sitting in full view. You may have to dig underground and study the roots to determine the cause of the trouble, or wait for night to catch such creatures as slugs.

Pests which attack leaves and flowers are the most easily identified because the damage occurs rapidly and is usually quite recognizable. Two main groups of pests attack leaves: those which have biting mouthparts (for example, beetles) and those with sucking mouthparts (such as greenfly). They may hide inside or outside the leaves or, like the notorious leaf-miner, burrow between the middle layers of leaf tissue.

Larger pests (like caterpillars) are usually more noticeable but they may attack and run (or fly) away, in which case you should spray, or lay bait, against the next visit.

Fortunately there are many methods of control at your fingertips, providing you diagnose the enemy correctly and act as swiftly as you can.

Understanding the enemy
Knowing something about the life cycles and habits of pests can help you in anticipating and preventing trouble. For instance, a major factor in determining how active they are is temperature; the warmer it becomes the busier they get. And up to 35°C (95°F) they breed faster too. Cold winters greatly decrease the numbers overwintering in the garden.

Opposite: early spring spraying will help control pests and diseases. Left: fly agaric growing near a birch tree damaged by rabbits. Below: common green capsid (Lygocoris pabulinus), *found on trees, shrubs and perennials.*

PESTS – a guide to treatment

PLACE	COMMON PESTS	PLANT AREA	TREATMENT	OTHER ADVICE
GREENHOUSE PLANTS	Aphids Whitefly	Leaves Stems Flowers	Treat as for house plants or fumigate greenhouse with nicotine, dichlorvos or BHC.	Make sure all vents are closed while fumigating. Do not enter until fumes have dispersed.
	Scale insect	Leaves	Wipe off, but if badly infested spray with malathion, nicotine or systemic insecticides.	Scrape insects off where possible.
	Red spider mite	Leaves	Spray malathion, derris or pyrethrum.	Pick off and burn badly infected leaves.
	Mealy bug	Leaves Stems	Spray with systemic or non-systemic insecticides.	Scrape insects off where possible.
	Leaf hopper	Leaves	Spray with BHC, malathion or nicotine, often available in aerosol or smoke form.	
	Leaf miner	Leaves	Spray with BHC or malathion.	Pick and burn infected leaves.
	Vine weevil	Roots	Remove and destroy grubs found when repotting plants. Drench soil of infected plants with BHC solution.	Incorporate naphthalene or paradichlorbenzene among the crocks when known susceptible plants are repotted.
HOUSE PLANTS	Aphids Whitefly	Leaves Stems Flowers	Non-systemic sprays: eg derris, pyrethrum, are often sufficient. For bad attacks use systemics, eg dimethoate.	Check all newly acquired potted plants and eradicate any pests to prevent them spreading among your existing plants.
	Mealy bug	Leaves Stems	Spray with systemic or non-systemic insecticides, or dab with methylated spirit.	Scrape insects off where possible.
	Scale insect	Leaves	Wipe with a soft cloth dipped in soapy water or methylated spirits, or treat as for aphids and whitefly.	Place your house plants in the greenhouse when you fumigate and do both jobs at once.
	Leaf hopper	Leaves	Spray with BHC, malathion or nicotine (often available in aerosol form).	
	Leaf miner	Leaves	Spray with BHC or malathion.	Pick and burn infected leaves.
	Vine weevil	Roots	See GREENHOUSE PLANTS	
FLOWER GARDEN	Aphids Whitefly	Leaves Stems Flowers	Spray with systemic insecticide such as dimethoate or formothion.	Malathion is also effective.
	Scale insect	Leaves Stems	Spray with malathion or systemic insecticide.	Scrape off insects where possible.
	Earwigs	Flowers	Reduce populations by spraying with BHC or trichlorphon prior to flowering.	Place inverted, straw-filled flower pot traps on 1m (3 ft) canes near plants; burn resulting earwig nests.
	Capsid bug	Leaves Stems Flowers	Spray with BHC or malathion as soon as damage appears.	Prompt action is essential.

PLACE	COMMON PESTS	PLANT AREA	TREATMENT	OTHER ADVICE
VEGETABLE GARDEN	Caterpillars	Leaves	Spray or dust with BHC, malathion or derris.	Pick caterpillars off where possible.
	Cutworm	Roots Stems	Work BHC dust or bromophos into the soil when planting.	Prevention is better than cure.
	Slugs Snails	Leaves Stems	Spray or apply pellets of methaldehyde or methiocarb.	These pests usually attack at night.
	Pea/bean weevil Grubs Thrips	Leaves Pods Peas	Apply BHC dust or fenitrion.	Apply when first flowers open and again 2 weeks later.
	Flea beetle	Leaves	Apply BHC dust when sowing seeds and at seedling stage.	Keep seedlings covered with dust until true leaves appear.
	Aphids	Leaves Shoots	Spray with systemic insecticides or malathion.	Watch for a reinfestation.
	Whitefly	Leaves	Spray with pyrethrum, dimethoate or BHC.	Malathion is also effective.
	Cabbage-root fly Carrot fly	Roots	Dust or spray BHC.	Keep seedlings covered with dust until true leaves appear.
FRUIT GARDEN	Caterpillars	Leaves	Spray or dust with BHC, malathion or derris.	Pick caterpillars off where possible.
	Aphids	Leaves Shoots	Spray with a systemic insecticide.	Watch for a reinfestation.
	Woolly aphids	Stems	Spray malathion or a systemic insecticide.	Systemic insecticides can be used, but at least 21 days before harvesting.
	Maggots	Fruits	Spray fenitrothion, BHC or derris.	Spray twice, in mid and late summer, as prevention.
	Gooseberry sawfly	Leaves	Spray thoroughly with derris or malathion.	Attacks usually occur in early summer.
	Capsid bug	Leaves Fruits	Spray with BHC or malathion as soon as damage is noted.	Prompt action is essential.
	Red spider mite	Leaves	Spray malathion, derris or pyrethrum, or a systemic.	Spray systemics 21 days before picking.
FLOWER GARDEN continued	Caterpillars	Flowers	Spray with BHC or trichlorphon.	Pick caterpillars off by hand.
	Leaf miner	Leaves	Spray with BHC or malathion or use systemic insecticide.	Pick off and burn badly infected leaves.
	Frog hopper (Cuckoo spit)	Leaves Stems	Spray with malathion, BHC, derris or pyrethrum.	Can be washed off with spray of soapy water.
	Slugs Snails	Leaves Stems	Spray or apply pellets of methaldehyde or pyrethrum.	These pests are most active at night.
	Thrips	Flowers	Spray pyrethrum.	Prompt action is important.
	Red spider mite	Leaves	Spray malathion, derris or pyrethrum.	Pick off and burn badly-infected leaves.

Above: always use protective clothing when handling insecticides and follow the manufacturer's instructions.

Day length also plays a part in controlling the breeding seasons and migration patterns of many insects. This is why they always become scarce in autumn, even before cold weather arrives. Clear away and burn garden refuse every autumn because it provides ideal shelter for overwintering pests. Many overwinter as eggs which can also be destroyed by the use of insecticides.

Use of insecticides

Most pesticides are sold under trade names, partly because the chemical names and formulae are cumbersome and difficult to remember. You can, however, be sure of getting the right product by reading the contents on the label and checking with the chemical, or proper, name given here. Full chemical names are often abbreviated – for instance, benzene hexachloride is known as BHC. (It is also sometimes called gamma-BHC.)

Always use protective clothing. Rubber gloves are important and be sure always to wash hands and face thoroughly after using insecticides. Never allow children or animals to be with you when sprays are being applied, and don't let them eat anything that has just been sprayed. Also wash out all spraying equipment after use—but not in the kitchen sink.

In some cases you may be able to use physical methods of combat such as picking caterpillars off plants and burning them. These are always preferable to spraying, because all sprays have some adverse effect on the plant. This is why you must adhere strictly to the manufacturer's recommended rate of application and wear protective clothing when handling insecticides.

How insecticides work

Insecticides kill in two main ways; first, as a stomach poison, when the pest either eats it with the leaf or sucks it up with the plant sap. Alternatively, if the pest is sprayed directly, the chemical will poison through the 'skin' or suffocate the pest. The method you choose depends on several factors, such as climate, type of insect and type of plant involved.

Non-systemic ('knock-down') insecticides

Many early insecticides killed either by blocking the breathing processes or by poisoning when absorbed through other exterior surfaces. But they did not persist for long and had to be used frequently in order to be effective. However, some are still very useful for certain purposes.

Pyrethrum and derris, for example, are both very effective general insecticides. They are derived from plants and do not persist for long. This means they are safe to use on vegetables—even up to the day before harvesting. Derris, however, is harmful to fish so do not use it near stocked pools.

But DDT, used by gardeners for so many years, has now been withdrawn from the gardening market as other, newer insecticides have proved to be safer and equally (if not more) efficient. Trichlorphon is one good modern substitute for DDT.

Systemic insecticides The systemics are absorbed by the plant and dispersed throughout its entire system; any biting or sucking insect will ingest them while feeding and be killed. These pest-killers remain in the plant for several days (sometimes even weeks) and they act against a wide variety of pests.

But too often spraying can result in the development of pests that are resistant to them. So spray on sighting the enemy rather than 'just in case'.

Dimethoate and formothion are systemic insecticides that control most aphids, red spider mite, scale insect, mealy bug, caterpillars and leaf hoppers. Systemic insecticides are also one of the most successful ways of killing many of the root-feeding insects, such as lettuce root aphid.

Above: waterlogging can result after heavy rain if a soil contains too much clay.

DISEASES AND DISORDERS

Although categorized together in this book with pests, diseases work in quite a different way. Like humans and other animals, plants are prone to various diseases that weaken, disfigure or destroy. These diseases may be separated into two groups; 1 parasites, ie viruses, fungi, bacteria, and 2, non-parasites, ie functional disorders due to mineral deficiencies and environmental factors such as waterlogging, drought and air pollution. Parasites work within the plant, absorbing its food supply, weakening and sometimes killing in the process, eg honey fungus, or causing stunting and malformations, eg several viruses. These more deadly parasitic diseases are difficult to eradicate without killing the plant in the process. Viruses in particular come into this category (though plants can be freed from them by special heat treatment carried out by laboratory techniques).

Non-parasitic factors may initially work externally, eg waterlogging and drought may rot or upset the root system, leading to stunting, wilting or leaf-fall. Air pollution may also bring about premature leaf-fall or scorch symptoms. Lack of essential minerals works internally, upsetting the physiology of the plant, eg lack of potash in fruit trees may cause die-back of shoots (or in redcurrants, death of leaf margins—known as marginal scorch), while manganese deficiency results in a striking yellow suffusion or variegation. It is important, therefore, to make sure there are no drainage problems and that plants do not lack water in times of drought. If a healthy soil is maintained (see Chapter 1) by regular mulching with, or digging in, decayed manure, garden compost, leaf mould, etc, most, if not all, of the necessary minerals will also be added and deficiencies will rarely or never occur.

Fungus diseases

Fungi, bacteria and viruses are the three main causes of plant disease, and of these the most important to the gardener are the fungi. Unlike insects, they can only live in and with the plant they infect, and they are common in all plants, large or small – from the tiniest seedling affected by 'damping-off' to the tall and sturdy elm tree laid low by Dutch elm disease.

Although it is quite often a simple matter to recognise that a plant is diseased – discoloration, distortion of growth, even a general air of listlessness, are all easily observed symptoms – it is usually much harder to diagnose exactly what is wrong with it. It is important, therefore, to learn to recognize the different kinds of fungal infection, so that the right remedies can be applied where possible and without delay.

Above: inkcaps growing on a lawn. Below: a spore cloud puffed from the earthstar Geastrum triplex.

Below: an all too familiar sight—a dead elm killed by the fungus Ceratocystis ulmi, *spread by elm-bark beetles.*

Propagation of fungi Most fungi propagate by microscopic spores (which are very similar in kind, although not in appearance, to the seeds of plants), and these can be carried from plant to plant by the wind, rain, soil or plant debris, animals and birds, and other means. Each fungus will produce many spores, and this is one of the reasons why they spread so quickly through a bed of plants, a greenhouse, or a whole garden.

Other fungi, and particularly those that attack roots, spread by means of mycelium (a fibrous growth that has much the same function as the roots or stems of plants).

The majority of fungi spread and do most damage in moist, warm conditions. To reduce the likelihood of fungal infection of roots, therefore, it is important to keep the soil well drained; and in the greenhouse adequate ventilation is essential. However, some fungi (of which the powdery mildews are an outstanding example) prefer drier conditions.

Physiological disorders

Not all plant troubles are caused by pests and diseases. Some are due to physiological disorders brought about by such factors as heat, cold, drought, waterlogging and pollution. Disease-like symptoms are also caused by insufficient quantities of one or more soil minerals essential for balanced growth. In addition to the basic nitrogen (nitrates), potassium (potash) and phosphorus (phosphate) (the NPK of general fertilizers), there are several other mineral salts essential for plant growth. Some of these are needed only in minute amounts and are known as trace elements or micro-nutrients. Well known examples of deficiencies are boron which causes brown crack of celery and brown heart of turnips, and magnesium, causing leaf yellowing between the veins followed by premature leaf fall in fruit trees and other woody plants. Applying the missing element to the root system or leaves, soon corrects the disease-like symptoms.

WEEDS AND THEIR CONTROL

Although a nuisance in the garden, weeds provide a problem quite different from that of pests and diseases. They are a group of plants, usually of no decorative value, which compete with and may overwhelm the garden favourites. Weeds have a variety of origins. The commonest kinds are wild plants which have evolved to take advantage of open or new habitats, eg land newly emerged from beneath an ice-sheet or scoured by fire, water or volcanic eruption. Such plants need to be tenacious and are therefore good potential weeds. Many weeds can only survive while they have plenty of light and room to grow. Once the site is overgrown with shrubs or trees they disappear. Most annual weeds owe their success to a phenomenal speed of growth, germinating and reaching the flowering state in a few weeks and producing seeds that mature very quickly. Sometimes an introduced ornamental plant takes advantage of a good soil and the lack of close competition to which it was adapted in the wild and behaves like a weed. Japanese knotweed is a classic example, but most sorts of mint, soapwort *(Saponaria officinalis)* and snow-in-summer *(Cerastium tomentosum)* are perhaps more familiar. How a plant behaves largely depends upon soil type and climate. In most soils for example, water-loving plants such as Japanese butturbur *(Petasites japonicus)* can soon be a major nuisance. In dry soils it barely thrives. In mild winter areas several of the bulbous-rooted *Oxalis* species can also be serious weeds. The Bermuda buttercup *(O. pes-caprae)* is one of these, but in frosty winter areas it is soon killed out.

So what is a weed? The short answer to that question is: any plant growing where it is not wanted. For instance, a grape seedling germinating in your dahlia bed is a weed – unless you want a vine amongst the dahlias. In a stricter sense, weeds are the native ancestors of our cultivated garden plants; they are undesirable because they are less attractive, generally bear smaller flowers or fruits, and are more vigorous in competition with their descendants. Weeds compete for water, nutrients and light, and often deprive cultivated plants, especially the seedlings and young ones, of their fair share of these necessities, because the

Opposite: there is no room for weeds in this garden. Right: weeds take over a neglected back garden.

Above left: an onion bed invaded by a variety of weeds including speedwell and scarlet pimpernel. Above right: an onion hoe helps keep Brussels sprouts free of weeds.

weeds adapt better to less favourable conditions.

There are two basic types of weeds – perennial and annual: the former are far harder to eliminate.

Perennial weeds
Most perennial weeds are quick-growing and tenacious, often re-growing from roots or rootstocks. They are, therefore, very difficult to get rid of. Herbaceous types, such as couch grass, bindweed (convolvulus and calystegia species) and ground elder are often notoriously deep-rooted. They store food in their fleshy roots, rhizomes, stolons, tubers or bulbs. It is easy to remove the visible vegetation but difficult to eradicate the roots. With woody plants, such as brambles and ivy, it is harder to get rid of the growth above ground, but comparatively easy to eradicate the roots, which must be burnt.

Manual weeding Good hand-weeding is still one of the best ways to rid yourself of perennial weeds. Some well-timed work with a trowel will save you much time and trouble later on – providing you don't leave any of the roots in the soil.

If working near decorative or vegetable plants where you don't want to use chemical weedkillers, then manual weeding becomes a necessity. You may need to use a fork, trowel, knife or even a mattock (like a pickaxe). Be careful that you don't just carve them up; this merely helps to propagate them and makes more work in the future. Dig up the weeds, complete with roots, and then burn them or put them in the dustbin.

When cultivating fresh ground it is essential to remove all the roots and underground storage systems; although hard work, it pays to lift them out by hand. Don't use a rotary cultivator on couch grass or dock-infested land as it will only chop up the weeds and encourage regrowth. Hoeing can have the same effect on a smaller scale unless you take care to remove the root, not just chop off leaves.

Weedkillers Weedkillers are categorized according to their mode of action, so that you can buy whichever is most suited to your needs.

TOTAL In an area devoid of decorative or culinary plants you can use a 'total' weedkiller, such as aminotriazole, to 'sweep the board'. A total weedkiller will kill all plants with which it comes into contact. You must take great care not to let it drift onto other plants or onto your neighbour's property. There have been many skirmishes over the garden wall as a result of misapplied weedkillers. After using it, remove and burn the debris and plant nothing in the ground for two to three months. If treatment with a total weedkiller is followed by a dose of a residual weedkiller (such as simazine) you will have a weed-free site for several months.

Another total weedkiller is sodium chlorate. It has to be used with great care as it spreads in the soil and can kill plants some distance away from the spot it was applied. Another danger is that, mixed with many other substances, it may be spontaneously inflammable, and it is therefore dangerous to store. It has a residual effect for up to a year.

Total and residual weedkillers are best for clearing paths and driveways.

RESIDUAL OR PRE-EMERGENT
These will not kill established weeds but they help to prevent the germination of most weeds for up to three months. There are various degrees of persistence.

Simazine has a long persistence, but it can be harmful to some shrubs (such as deutzia). Propachlor lasts for shorter periods but is less toxic.

This type remains in a narrow band of the topsoil, so that any weed seeds germinating in this zone take up the chemical and die. It is possible to apply residual weedkiller where bulbs are planted, because their roots are located below the weedkiller band, and they grow quickly through it without suffering any damage. Plants such as runner beans, sweet peas, daffodils and hyacinths will all grow through the weedkiller layer after it has become inactive.

SELECTIVE Some weedkillers are termed 'selective' as they kill dicotyledons (broad-leaved plants), but will not damage many monocotyledons – such as grasses. Selective onces like 2,4-D, MCPA, 2,4,5-T or fenoprop (hormone types) kill by causing the plant to overgrow its food reserves so that it literally grows itself to death. Use this kind with great care as the slightest drift will damage crops; tomatoes are especially sensitive to them.

NON-SELECTIVE The well-known paraquat and diquat weedkillers will only kill perennial weeds while they are still at seedling stage. After a few weeks they become immune and these preparations merely burn off their foliage and allow

Spraying and dusting equipment

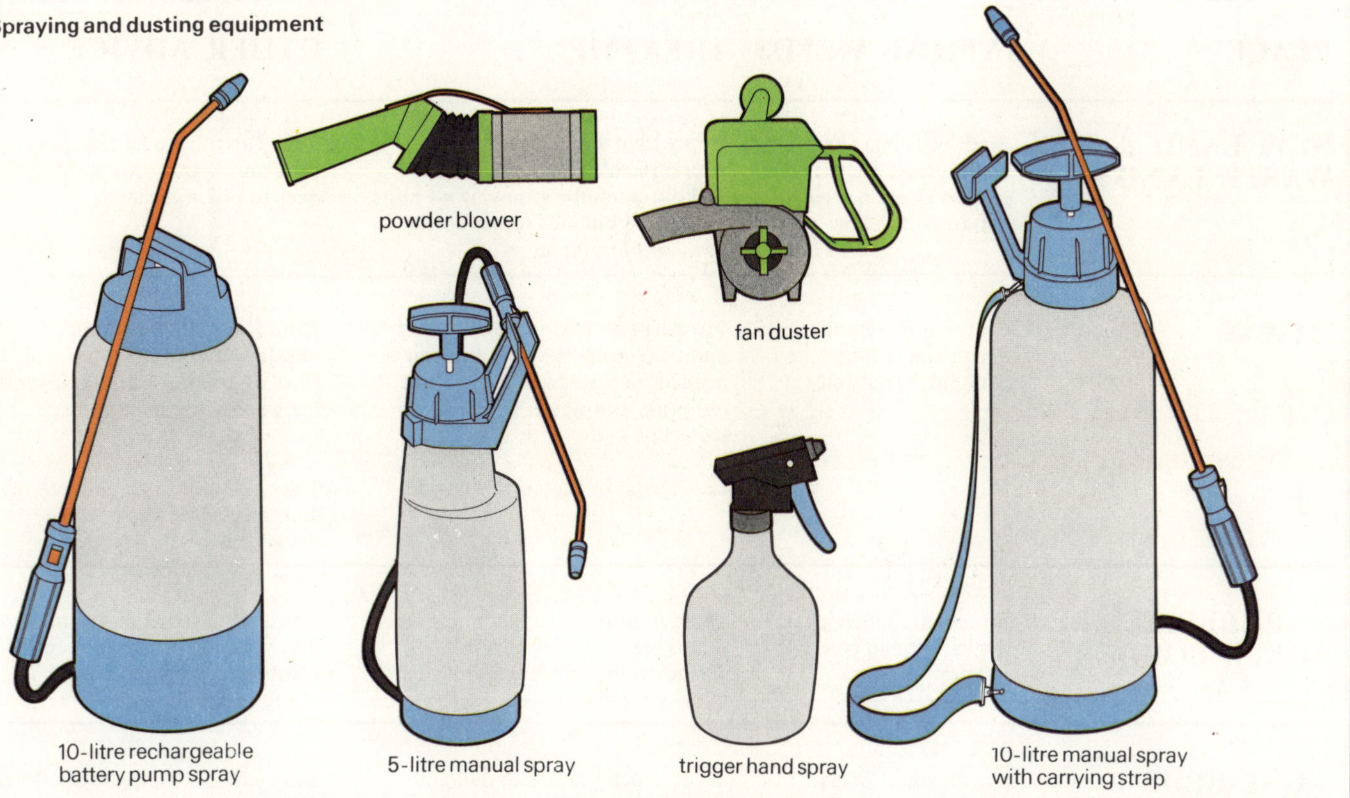

the roots to re-grow. They are deactivated immediately they meet the soil and are therefore safe to use provided they do not drift. But they must be kept away from children and animals: under no circumstances store them in old lemonade or other misleading bottles.

Methods of application Always read the maker's instructions on the package and follow them closely; they have been based on years of research. Our recommendations give the chemical name, so when buying proprietary brands check the package label and see that it contains the correct constituents for your purpose. Keep a separate watering can for use with chemical weedkillers, and use a rose fitting or dribble-bar attachment for controlled application.

A good way to minimize drift is to make up a solution of chemical weedkiller in a container and dip the tips of the weeds in it. This will then be taken up through the plant by the sap stream – and kill it. You may need to make several applications over a few days for them to be effective. This method also works on many wild, shrubby plants such as dog rose and ivy (*Hedera helix*).

Annual weeds

Annual weeds, by definition, mature, flower, seed and die within one year. 'Seed' is the operative word here, because this is the method by which they reproduce and infest the garden. It is also the key to their control; if you can remove the seed before it reaches the soil you can stop the next generation of weeds before it starts.

Weeding by hoeing One of the most common, and time-honoured, ways of controlling annual weeds is by hoeing. The secret of successful hoeing is to choose a day that is dry, sunny and, preferably, has a steady breeze. All these factors help to dry out the weed seedlings on the soil surface and prevent them re-rooting.

Don't just decapitate the weeds when you hoe; make sure the roots are removed.

In a way, you make extra work for yourself by hoeing because you constantly bring more weed seeds to the surface where they germinate. Seeds can remain viable in the ground for years, waiting until they come near to the surface before starting to grow. Some seeds are very sensitive to the amount of daylight available and can only spring into life when they are in the topmost layer of soil. Regular hoeing, however, will keep weed seedlings under control.

Controlling with weedkillers Most annual weeds are more easily controlled by weedkillers than their perennial

Above: spraying and dusting equipment.
Below: a well kept lawn.

PERENNIAL WEEDS – a guide to treatment

PLACE	TYPICAL WEEDS	TREATMENT	OTHER ADVICE
NEW LAND & WASTE LAND	Bindweed; blackberry; couch grass; docks; ivy; ground elder; nettles; oat-grass; thistles	Apply total weedkiller, eg aminotriazole; clear away debris and dig carefully, removing all roots, tubers and bulbous roots. Throw away or burn these.	Take care not to let the spray drift on to your own plants or over to other gardens.
LAWNS	Creeping buttercup; daisy; dandelion; plantain; speedwell	Mowing and raking; apply 2,4-D and mecoprop mixtures (ioxynil is needed for speedwell). Lever out old grass and weeds with a sharp trowel or knife.	Do not use 2,4-D or mecoprop on new lawns until the grass is at least six months old; use ioxynil for weeds on young lawns.
	Moss	Lawn sand or mercuric chloride.	Take care not to let children or animals near either of these dangerous poisons.
SHRUBBERIES & MIXED BORDERS	Bindweed; couch grass; docks; ground elder; thistles	Dig out all roots; apply a residual weedkiller to prevent fresh germination; dichlobenil kills many perennial weeds.	Check all instructions to make sure that your borders do not contain plants that are sensitive to some of the residual weedkillers.
ROSE BEDS	Couch grass; many germinating perennials	Treat couch grass with dalapon and remove by hand; simazine will prevent germination and dichlobenil completely kills many of these perennial weeds.	Take care not to let weedkiller get on to roses, especially if in leaf; apply simazine in early spring to last through most of the plant-growing season.
HERBACEOUS & FLOWER BORDERS	Many germinating and established weeds	Propachlor is a good residual weedkiller to check further germination, provided all established weeds are removed by hand or fork first.	Ensure that weather is warm and soil moist before applying propachlor.
FRUIT	Established and germinating perennials (especially couch grass and creeping buttercup in strawberries)	Use diquat or paraquat between rows to kill new weeds; dalapon for couch grass; dichlobenil for established weeds; simazine residual weedkiller around trees, bush and cane fruit.	Dig out weeds from strawberry plants as they are very sensitive to weedkillers, especially when in full leaf.
VEGETABLES	All weeds	Don't let weeds get too large before treatment. Hoe frequently to remove germinating weeds; use propachlor for some crops, but check instructions first to ensure safety of growing plants.	Hoeing is best done on warm days as weeds die from exposure and will not re-root in soil tilth; pull out any large weeds after a shower of rain.
PATHS & DRIVES	All weeds	Apply a total weedkiller, such as aminotriazole, sodium chlorate or simazine.	Avoid contact with cultivated plants in the vicinity.

counterparts. A whole range of annuals succumb to applications of dichlobenil or propachlor. Both these weedkillers are residual, but last only a few months. Diquat and paraquat are very useful for killing germinating weed seedlings. You can spot apply these anywhere provided you take care not to let them drift onto other plants.

Unlike many perennials, annual weeds germinate within the narrow soil-surface band to which the weedkillers have been applied; therefore they die almost as soon as they start growing. So, on the whole, these weedkillers tend to be more effective against annuals. Always remember where these chemicals have been put down and make sure that no horticultural activities 'break the band' as this will allow the weeds to come through unscathed.

Food crops

Broadly speaking the chemical weedkillers that are used in the vicinity of food crops can be divided into those that kill through the leaves and those that kill through the roots. Both types are equally effective but their efficiency and usefulness depend on their being used in the right places, at the right times and at the correct strength.

Do not use sodium chlorate – even though it is one of the oldest and most popular of weedkillers. It is an efficient destroyer of plant life, but it does have serious disadvantages. It is fully soluble in water and, when applied to a given area, will spread sideways, endangering other nearby plants. It remains potent in the ground for a considerable time until it is eventually washed out of the soil by rain.

On heavy soils its enduring toxicity makes it unsafe to plant anything for up to a year and even on light, sandy soils the ground must be left fallow for three months or more. So do not use it on the vegetable plot or on the ground around it.

Weedkillers containing simazine are also total root-entering killers but, unlike sodium chlorate, they are not soluble and merely go into suspension when added to water. This means that they do not spread and their destructiveness is confined to the zone of application. You can, therefore, apply them to paths without fear of their toxicity spreading into the food-growing areas.

Then there are the weedkillers containing a chemical called paraquat that revolutionized gardening when it was first introduced. Paraquat kills through the leaves by destroying their internal cell structure and rendering them incapable of sustaining life. It has no effect whatsoever on the soil and is rendered harmless on contact with it. This means that paraquat will only kill what it touches and therefore its application can be accurately controlled. You can use it safely to kill weeds between rows of vegetables providing it does not come into contact with the vegetable leaves.

Unfortunately paraquat can be lethal to humans as well as to plants and you must treat it with great caution. Always wear rubber gloves and wash your face and hands thoroughly when the job is done. Wash the can out, several times, to make sure that all chemical residues are dispersed. You should keep a special watering can for all chemical weedkillers so that you cannot, through error or carelessness, harm your plants with contaminated liquid.

Lawn weeds and their control

The ready availability of mosskillers and selective weedkillers means that the fine-leaved grasses essential for a high-quality lawn can now grow freely, without fear of competition from undesirable elements.

There is a wide selection of lawn weedkillers and mosskillers on the market. Here we describe the main choices, and their respective uses.

Broad-leaved weeds The appearance of so-called 'hormone' weedkillers in the late 1940s revolutionized the control of weeds such as daisies, plantains, dandelions and buttercups. These chemicals introduced a completely new concept of control in that they were capable of killing broad-leaved weeds without damaging narrow-leaved grasses. Consequently, it was possible to weed by the simple expedient of watering them, in solution, on to the lawn.

Hormone weedkillers The first of this new class of killer was MCPA, followed soon after by 2,4-D. Later a whole series of variants was introduced, including mecoprop, fenoprop and dichlorprop. Although all these behave in a similar fashion, each has its own special virtues. Thus MCPA and 2,4-D while very effective against daisies, plantains, dandelions and buttercups, have little effect on white clover, chickweed and pearlwort. Mecoprop, fenoprop and dichlorprop, on the other hand, give excellent results against these resistant weeds. Consequently, modern lawn weedkillers usually contain MCPA or 2,4-D combined with mecoprop, fenoprop or dichlorprop. Dicamba is another weedkiller that is available as a mixture with 2,4-D.

These chemicals all act by stimulating the weeds into deformed and excessive growth, so treated weeds at first appear

Below: the dandelion can be effectively removed.

more prominent. However, the killing action is quite slow and can continue for up to six weeks. If a repeat treatment is needed to obtain complete control, it should be delayed six to eight weeks after the first application.

APPLICATION Since the killing action takes the form of a growth response, the use of killers needs to be restricted to the period from late spring to mid autumn (late April to September), during which the weeds are growing actively. These treatments should not be given in cold weather or during periods of drought when weed growth is at a low level.

Weedkillers are commonly applied as solutions, using a watering can fitted with a normal rose. The rose can be replaced by a sprinkle-bar that not only makes it easier to apply the solution evenly, but also enables the job to be done with less water. Pressure sprayers can be used provided they are adjusted to give a coarse spray, but even then there is the risk of damage being caused to nearby cultivated plants by spray drift. Never apply weedkiller on a windy day.

It is not essential to use weedkillers in a solution. A combined granular feed/weed product, making it possible to feed and weed the lawn in one operation, is an alternative approach.

Although few lawns are entirely free of weeds, in many cases the infestation is too light to justify overall treatment. In this situation one of the proprietary aerosol spot-weedkillers provides the easy answer, producing a narrow jet of liquid that is easily aimed at individual weeds. Furthermore, some of the products are designed to cover the treated weeds with foam, making it easy to see those that have been treated.

LIMITATIONS Provided they are used as the manufacturers recommend, selective weedkillers have no ill effects on established grass. However, they can be very damaging to bulbs such as daffodils, and plants with grass-like leaves. So areas of lawn with naturalized bulb plantings should not be treated till the bulb foliage has died down and been mown off.

One limitation of hormone weedkillers is that, while they can safely be used on established lawns, they can be damaging to seedling grass or newly-turfed lawns. Should weeding be necessary in these areas, then the chemical to use is ioxynil; this is also effective against highly-resistant weeds such as speedwell (veronica) in established lawns, particularly if mixed with 2,4-D.

Weed grasses Lawns are constantly subject to invasions by strong-growing weed grasses like Yorkshire fog and creeping soft-grass. These clump-forming wild grasses are readily recognized by their broad leaves and silvery, hairy appearance. Selective weedkillers have no effect on these weeds. Instead, the clumps should be cut out with a knife and the lawn level made up with fresh soil. Small areas will fill in with growth from the lawn grasses; larger areas may need to be re-seeded.

Mosses and Lichens Infestation by mosses is a recurrent problem with many lawns. These primitive plants are naturally among the first invaders of bare, undisturbed ground, and can quickly colonize bare patches caused by too-close mowing, or indeed any area where the grass is sparse. Lawns that are heavily shaded or poorly drained are particularly prone to invasion.

Moss on a lawn is usually at its most obvious in the spring. This is because it is able to continue growing during the winter when grass growth is minimal. Late spring (April) is the best time to use a mosskiller, since the grass is then able to grow into the spaces.

LAWN SAND One method of controlling moss is to apply lawn sand: this consists of sulphate of iron and sulphate of ammonia, bulked out with sand. This mixture needs to be applied very carefully as it can be damaging to the grass.

OTHER MOSSKILLERS A modern alternative is to use one of the proprietary killers; these also contain sulphate of iron, but they have no ill effects on the grass. Indeed, these products make the lawn look more attractive by giving it a greener colour, and they also supply nitrogen, thus stimulating early growth of the grass.

In addition to sulphate of iron, there are a number of other chemicals used in proprietary lawn mosskillers. These include chloroxuron, dichlorophen, mercurous chloride (calomel) and tar oil. All these, when used as directed, will kill moss, but none of them stimulates grass to better growth.

Above: lawn moss is best destroyed in late spring, since the grass can then grow in the space left.

A lichen *Peltigera canina* is sometimes found growing on lawns on acid, sandy soil. It forms brownish, leafy lobes that make dense, unsightly clumps. Mosskillers are effective against it, but the fertility of the soil should also be improved by the use of fertilizers, in order to reduce the risk of re-invasion.

Controlling with ground-cover

In ornamental areas of the garden the aim should be to get a complete cover of the soil with the cultivated plants so that few weeds can get a footing. This is the philosophy behind the ground-cover approach to gardening and works very well provided the soil is free of perennial weeds to begin with and the plants are placed close enough together to touch each other in one, or at the most, two, growing seasons. In the interim, hand-weeding will be necessary.

Weed biology

Getting to know the weeds of one's own garden, especially in their early stages, is well worthwhile. Knowing the correct name of weed seedlings means that the most efficient treatment can be undertaken before it becomes a real nuisance. Seedlings are more easy to kill than established plants, especially the deep-rooted perennials.

At all costs, weeds must be removed or killed by herbicides before they seed. The old saying 'One year's seeding means seven year's weeding', has been confirmed experimentally. About half of all freshly

Top left: creeping thistle (Cirsium arvense). *Top right: sow thistle* (Sonchus asper).

Bottom left: chickweed (Stellaria media). *Bottom centre: red dead nettle* (Lamium purpureum). *Bottom right: annual nettle* (Urtica urens).

shed seed germinates during the first twelve months, a half of the remainder the following year and so on. Much depends on the actual weed species and number of seeds present in the soil. Assuming that 1,000 seeds per sq m (100 per sq ft) are present—a not infrequent occurrence—about seven years will elapse before all have germinated. If there are as many as 10,000 seeds per sq m (over 900 seeds per sq ft), and this is by no means impossible, then about ten years will pass before all germinate. Digging weedy ground means that seeds are buried too deeply to grow. When the ground is dug at a later date, however, and they are brought to the surface, germination often occurs rapidly. Deeply buried seeds can last in a germinatable state anytime from 10-40 years or even longer. So preventing seeds from flowering and seeding is important in the battle against them.

Identifying weeds
To aid identification, weeds can be divided into several sections with characteristics in common:

Perennials with prostrate, creeping stems
Slender speedwell, white clover, oxalis (yellow), creeping buttercup.

Perennials with creeping underground stems or roots which produce aerial stems
Yarrow, horsetail, knotweed (Japanese), thistle (creeping), bindweed (field and hedge), ground elder, bellflower (creeping), winter heliotrope, yellow cress (creeping), coltsfoot, willowherb, dead nettle (white).

Plants with leaves divided into three leaflets
Clover, trefoil, medick and oxalis.

Plants with leaves divided into five or more leaflets
Buttercup (creeping), bittercress, ground elder, nipplewort, yellow cress (creeping), fumitory, poppy.

Leaves narrow, boldly lobed
Dandelion, shepherd's purse, sow thistles (all), groundsel. nipplewort, poppy.

Leaves finely cut
Yarrow, mayweeds, horsetail, fumitory, pineapple weed.

Leaves simple, roughly oval, toothed or not, sometimes pointed
Dead nettles, knotweed (Japanese), nettles (stinging), gallant soldier, bellflower (creeping), chickweed, miner's lettuce, mercury, nightshade (black), shepherd's purse, spurge (petty), dock (broad-leaved), plantain (greater), enchanters' nightshade, self-heal, fat hen.

Leaves simple, lance-shaped or narrower (grassy)
Plantain (ribwort), dock (curled), willow herbs, shepherd's purse, fleabane (Canadian), cleavers, pearlwort, grasses.

Leaves simple, roughly triangular in outline
Celandine (lesser), bindweed, fat hen, orache.

Leaves simple, rounded, with or without lobes
Coltsfoot, celandine (lesser), daisy, henbit, dead nettle (red), winter heliotrope, nipplewort.

Leaves in rosettes or flattened tufts, and with flowering stems arising directly from them
Daisy, dandelion, plantains.

Leaves simple, more or less spoon-shaped
Spurges (petty and sun), daisy, miner's lettuce.

Leaves with spines or stinging hairs
Thistles, nettles (true).

Leaves heart-shaped (included in oval-leaved)
Bellflower (creeping), nettles (true and dead), galland soldier, celandine (lesser), speedwell, winter heliotrope, enchanters' nightshade, self-heal.

PEST AND DISEASE CONTROL

If you are to have an attractive show of flowers and vegetables, pests, diseases and other troubles must be eliminated or reduced to a fairly harmless minimum.

Chemical control

Agricultural and horticultural chemists have provided a battery of chemicals designed to kill plants' enemies of all kinds.

Insecticides Substances used to kill insects that attack plants. Many different sorts are now known, ranging from the highly persistent organochlorine compounds – HCH – to simple extracts of derris roots and pyrethrum flowers. Some are of general use, others more specific. They are applied in several ways: as a liquid sprayed over infected plants to coat the insects (contact); watered on to the soil and taken up in the sap (systemic); as a dust or in smoke from a pyrotechnic canister – this method is used only for greenhouse or stores. The more general insecticides can often kill insect, pest and natural predator alike, and many are harmful or lethal to fish and other animals; for these reasons they must not be used indiscriminately, and the maker's instructions should always be followed. In the garden it is usually possible to spray or dust only the infected plants, thus allowing predators such as ladybirds to survive elsewhere.

Fungicides Substances used to check or kill fungal diseases. Fungi are also plants, although of a very primitive nature, their thread-like hyphae lacking chlorophyll, and it is difficult to find a substance that will kill the fungus but not the infected plant. The main standbys are still copper salts and sulphur in various forms, but they cannot be used on all plants, as they sometimes cause scorch or leaf-fall. Research over the past thirty years has now resulted in the manufacture of certain carbon compounds such as maneb and zineb, which, though rather specific in what they kill, do not damage the plant.

Biological control

Evolution has seen to it that there are control organisms for most plants and animals to prevent them from becoming too dominant. In turn these natural controls have their own controls or parasites. The situation was neatly summed up in verse by Jonathan Swift:

So, naturalists observe, a flea
Hath smaller fleas that on him prey;
And these have smaller still to bite 'em,
And so proceed *ad infinitum*.

Thus, with pests, one insect preys upon another and is in turn preyed upon. Sometimes this fact of life can be used to the gardener's benefit. Firstly it is wise, though not absolutely essential, to try to identify these beneficial insects. There are several useful field guides with good illustrations for the uninitiated. Most obvious among the beneficial insects are ladybirds, which feed on aphids of all sorts. Also with the same food preferences are hover-fly and lacewing-fly

Opposite: a healthy summer border.
Above left: a ladybird feeding off aphids.
Left: the larvae of a green lacewing attacking an aphid.

Above: Chrysopa carnea, *a green lacewing, at rest on an aphid-covered lettuce leaf, acts as a natural pest control.*

larvae (grubs). Ground, tiger and staphylinid beetles feed on caterpillars and other insects. Of even more importance are some of the parasite insects, the ichneumon flies, chalcid wasps and tachinid flies, the larvae of which live within the body of their host, killing it before maturity is reached. Regrettably, these natural enemies seldom give complete control and spraying may still be necessary. It should be done with care, however, and only on heavily-infected plants. Blanket-spraying destroys pest and predator alike, and when the pest develops an immunity to the spray – as frequently happens – a tremendous build-up can occur. More and more, it is being realized that a low level of pests held at bay by natural control is preferable to frequent expensive sprayings, the efficacy of which can break down at any time. Already biological control with this philosophy behind it is being effectively put to the test. In California, for example, a small ladybird has been bred in large quantities and released in orange orchards to control the scale insects. In Britain, the minute parasite *Encarsia formosa* is being used to control white-fly in greenhouses. For such methods to be a success the gardener will have to add a new facet to his techniques, that of caring for pest and predator alike and adjusting their build-ups. Sprays will still be needed for a long time to come, but hopefully in lessening amounts, for in the end it is best to work with, rather than against, nature.

The biological control of fungal and bacterial diseases is also being worked upon and is a promising aspect of control for the future. For example it has recently been discovered that the fungus *Verticillium lecanii* attacks certain rusts and mildews. There are several races of this fungus and one of them also parasitizes

Below: Syrphus *larva feeding on an aphid. Pale orange-yellow in colour, the larva is 20mm (¾in) long when full grown.*

aphids. Already this race is available in a limited way commercially but it is recommended for use only with chrysanthemums in greenhouses under humid conditions.

Non-parasitic situations are sometimes less easy to deal with. The important thing is to diagnose the trouble accurately and then to correct the cultural error or inadequacy, eg water regularly where drought symptoms prevail or add trace element fertilizers to the soil when a particular mineral is known to be deficient or absent.

Sprayers and dusters

To keep your plants and crops healthy you have to keep spraying at certain times to prevent—or counteract—the adverse effects of weeds, pests and diseases. It saves you time and trouble if you use the right spray for the job.

Many manufacturers of pesticides

Above: an adult female common yellow ophion (Ophion luteus)*, about 2cm (¾in) long. During the day this ichneumon wasp often rests on a leaf, becoming active at night. Left: a caterpillar of the large white butterfly festooned with the larvae of the ichneumon wasp.*

produce their chemicals in a pack which itself is the dispenser.

Dusts are sold in puffer-packs made of opaque polythene, with a small plastic nozzle-type orifice. To spray the dust you simply squeeze the sides of the pack. Other dust packs have pepper-pot tops.

Liquids are sometimes sold in inexpensive transparent plastic bottles with a manually-operated spray mechanism as the closure. It is not advisable to refill.

The most popular pack today is the aerosol can. This system is very effective and convenient to use, but must be stored away from heat.

Both aerosol sprays and dust packs are ideal for small gardens or limited applications, but prove very expensive for large areas or prolonged use.

Permanent sprayers The capacity range here goes from ½ litre (1 pt) to several litres. Sprayers over 5 litres (10 pt) capacity can be awkward and heavy to handle when full and are not recommended. On large areas it pays to refill, rather than struggle with a larger sprayer.

Traditionally, spraying equipment was made from metal and proved to be extremely heavy. Today, virtually all sprayers are made from lightweight but strong polythene and plastic with stainless metals in some of the working parts.

Trigger sprayers The smallest sprayers are suited for use on house plants, greenhouse plants and limited use outdoors. They are appropriately called hand sprayers because they are held in the hand and operated by simply pressing a trigger rather like a pistol. Naturally, the range of these models is limited and the operator has to be close to the plant.

Pump sprayers These consist of a container, a short length of hose and a lance. They require two hands for operation. The container is held in one hand while the lance is directed towards the target with the other hand. The spray container has a maintenance-free pump fitted through the top. The pump is primed by pushing in and pulling out the handle several times to build up pressure. Everything is then ready for spraying and all you do is depress a simple trigger fitted to the hand end of the lance.

Spray patterns are basically cone-shaped and are altered by rotating the nozzle fitment at the end of the lance.

Many of these sprayers have a useful shoulder strap so they may be carried around the garden with ease; this also allows you a free hand to pull the odd long branch or shoot out of the way. The carrying handle itself is usually dual purpose, enabling the lance to be slotted in when the sprayer is not in use.

Battery-operated sprays are convenient because they avoid the need for pressure-pumping. The batteries are rechargeable and sealed so they are not affected by wet weather. Life between charges is about 1½ hours. Units are made in 5 litre (10 pt) and 10 litre (20 pt) sizes.

Dusters Two types of dusting equipment are made: a cheap bellows type with handle which, when shaken, operates the bellows and expels the dust from the attached canister; and a more sophisticated piece of equipment in which you turn a geared handle to operate a fan and distribute the powder from a hopper.

CONTROLLING GREENHOUSE PESTS

Although pests and diseases are generally easier to control under glass than in the open, they will multiply and spread more freely unless you make routine checks and take prompt action. In addition, whereas winter in the outdoor garden is a fairly trouble-free time, many common pests and diseases can be troublesome all year round in the greenhouse.

A clean and tidy greenhouse will often deter many pests and diseases. By *not* storing rubbish and garden oddments there, you deprive pests of excellent hiding places, and by throwing away dead foliage and flowers you can discourage fungus diseases such as moulds, mildews and rusts. Make a daily inspection of the underside of the foliage; many pests and diseases make their first appearance here. Discard plants that are sickly for unknown reasons; they can endanger others.

Plants with pale or distorted flowers or foliage (sometimes stunted or mottled, or with striped blooms that fail to open properly) may be suffering from one or other of a number of virus diseases. These diseases can be spread by sap-sucking insects (like greenfly), by knives or scissors, or by your fingers. There is no cure for virus diseases and affected plants are best burned. Tomatoes are especially vulnerable, and ideally grown alone.

Flying pests Many familiar garden pests invade the greenhouse. Those that fly can enter through the vents. As a good preventive measure, fit screens of muslin to greenhouse vents in summer. This will stop butterflies and moths getting in; the eggs they lay may turn overnight into caterpillars that can do enormous damage before you spot them. Birds can also enter through the vents and may do much damage to plants, besides injuring themselves while trying to escape.

Crawling pests 'Creepy crawlies' may be brought indoors on the bottom of pots that have been standing in the garden. Slugs and snails are easily controlled by the usual baits used outdoors. These pests will often climb up the glass sides and gain access to pots and trays on the staging. Just one slug or snail can eat a whole tray of small seedlings during the night.

Never stand pots directly on the ground soil of the greenhouse (or outdoors). Stand them on sharp shingle, tile, stone or plastic. This prevents worms entering through the drainage holes. If

they do get in, the constant disturbance to the roots will make plants wilt.

Ants have a similar effect, but can be eradicated with a proprietary ant bait; there are several kinds (all very effective) on the market. Woodlice are not, as many believe, harmless to plants and they are especially damaging to seedlings. You will find these pests hiding among greenhouse rubbish. Dusts containing BHC will control them.

Earwigs can hide in the smallest cracks and crevices of the greenhouse structure. There they stay unseen during the day. At night they fly out (it is often not known that they can fly) and eat plants – flowers particularly – leaving the petals holed and ragged. Because they operate at night you may not realize that earwigs are the culprits, and the cause of the damage will remain a mystery. Chrysanthemums need special protection so use BHC dusts liberally. Ant bait is also often effective against earwigs, and can be put in possible hiding places.

Aphids and whitefly Aphids (or plant lice) are a group of insects that include greenfly and blackfly as well as numerous other closely related pests that suck plant sap. Few plants are safe from attack, so take routine preventive measures. Systemic pesticides give long-term protection under glass, and there are numerous quick-acting products now sold. Those containing malathion act very quickly, but the old-fashioned liquid derris pesticides are still efficient and very safe.

Above: fumigation protects against grey mould, a common infection in winter. Below: black garden ant worker with larvae (small white grubs) and pupae (the cocoons).

Whitefly has become a serious greenhouse pest. It often infests outdoor weeds, like nettles, and will then be a source of trouble to any nearby greenhouse in summer, and over winter in greenhouses that are free from frost. In appearance, the fly is minute, with pale grey wings. Like aphids, it sucks sap and also causes leaves and surfaces below them to become sticky with honeydew secretion. This often encourages a growth of black mould which, though not harmful, makes the plants look most unsightly.

Fortunately, a recently introduced pesticide called resmethrin is particularly effective for whitefly control, and generally useful for other similar pests. Apply it by spraying. Alternatively, malathion and BHC smokes can be used.

Thrips and red spider mite The tiny thrips cause foliage to become marked with whitish patches that are often encircled by dark specks. To check for their presence, put white paper below the foliage and then shake the leaves. The thrips fall off and you will be able to see them squirming against the white background. Most general pesticides will control thrips; systemics will be absorbed into the plant tissues and remain effective for a long time.

If, during summer, foliage becomes yellow and mottled and tends to fall, suspect a pest called red spider mite. If you look at the undersides of the leaves with a powerful magnifying glass, what you will see (if the pest is present) is a very tiny, mite-like creature and minute round, whitish eggs. In large and severe infestations the mites will show up as many thousands of pale-reddish 'spiders' spinning fine webbing. Since they enjoy hot, dry conditions, you can discourage them by keeping up humidity. Fumigation with azobenzene is very effective, but numerous greenhouse plants may be slightly damaged by this treatment, so be sure to check with the maker's label. Liquid extract of derris (not dusts) is a good general control if applied thoroughly.

Sciarid fly (fungus gnat) With the now widespread use of peat composts, sciarid fly maggots are becoming increasingly common. These are tiny, whitish, wriggling worms infesting the composts, or the peat spread over staging. There will also be tiny flies about – the 'worms' being their maggots. These maggots can do enormous harm to plant roots, especially seedlings, and may also eat lower parts of stems. Moist conditions encourage them. Water with a malathion insecticide, but try to keep moisture lower subsequently. The flies must be killed since they are the source of the trouble. Most general insecticides, such as HCH, malathion or pirimiphos-methyl, will do this.

Fungus diseases Two very common diseases caused by fungi are damping-off of seedlings and grey mould. If pricked-out seedlings topple over, it is a sure sign of damping-off. Always water in with Cheshunt compound as a precaution. Damping-off is less prevalent now that modern sterilized composts are used.

Below: black aphids and ants on broom. Right: yellow, mottled foliage in summer may indicate the presence of red spider mite. With severe infestations their fine webbing will be apparent.

Below: whitefly is a serious pest in the greenhouse, where it may overwinter if free from frost. The adult, with its pale grey wings, is easily recognizable.

Below: black aphids and ants on broom. Right: if conditions are hot and dry during the summer months, red spider mite can be a problem in the greenhouse, causing yellowing and mottling of leaves.

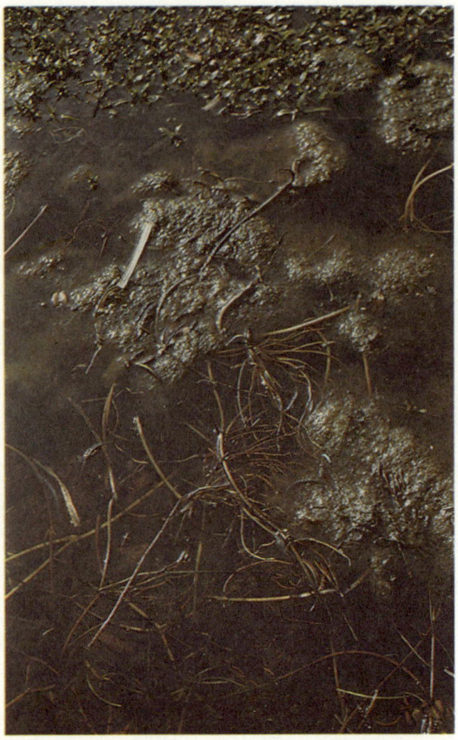

Left: a garden rake is useful for clearing weeds from the pond as it avoids having masses of dead weed decaying.
Above: blanketweed is usually associated with clear water and, in small quantities, is harmless. It can be killed chemically if necessary without harming other plant forms or fish by dosing the pond with a non-toxic algicide.

Grey mould (or botrytis) will attack both living and dead plant tissue. It is usually seen as a brownish-grey, furry mould which, if disturbed, distributes a cloud of fine 'dust' – the spores that spread the disease. On tomatoes the mould will cause flowers and fruit to drop, and fruit may be marked with small whitish rings with a black speck at the centre. Lettuce and chrysanthemums are especially prone to attack. To check the disease, increase ventilation and, at night, lower the humidity. Benlate sprays and TCNB fumigation are excellent controls and preventives of grey mould.

Using pesticides
Whenever possible, buy pesticides especially designed for greenhouse use. Read the labels carefully because some plants will be damaged by certain pesticides. In certain cases you can simply remove these plants from the greenhouse, or cover them with plastic bags, while other plants are being treated. Follow all safety precautions exactly (especially where edible crops are concerned) and, in the enclosed atmosphere of your greenhouse, take care that you do not inhale any pesticides yourself.

CONTROL OF PESTS AND DISEASES IN PONDS

One of the most fascinating aspects of water gardening is the variety of life that turns up from who-knows-where, and settles in as though the pond had been put there for just that purpose. Some of the uninvited guests (snails and leeches, for example) are undoubtedly introduced as eggs on the stems and leaves of water plants. Others arrive by air, among them blanketweed – the invisible spores of which drift in the atmosphere – and the midges and other winged insects that see the pond as an ideal spot for them to deposit their eggs.

Blanketweed (or silkweed)
This simple form of plant life makes tangled masses of long, silky threads. It is usually associated with very clear water, and since – like all green plants – it produces oxygen under the influence of light, it is harmless enough in small quantities. It thrives on sunlight and on mineral salts dissolved into the water. In a new pond in which the high mineral-salt content of the water is increased by minerals dissolved out of the planting soil, and with little surface cover to prevent maximum sunlight penetration, it may run riot and threaten to choke all other plant life.

Blanketweed can be killed chemically without harm to other plant forms or fish, but it is essential to remove as much as possible manually before treatment to avoid having masses of dead weed decaying in the pond. A rough stick twisted among the weed is remarkably effective in drawing strands from all parts of the pond to a central mass that can easily be lifted out. A spring-tine lawn rake is also very useful.

With the bulk of the weed removed to the compost heap, the remaining strands can be killed by dosing the pond with a

Above: a female *Chironomus* midge laying her eggs. The larvae of this and other species of midge are abundant in ponds, lakes and rivers; there are frequently many thousands to the square metre (yard). Right: the great diving beetle lives in the vegetation zone and is a voracious carnivore. Bottom: the underside of a water boatman.

non-toxic algicide such as Allclear or Algizin (P). This, of course, is first-aid treatment. The long-term solution is an abundance of oxygenating plants – azolla and hydrocharis, for example – and the leaves of water lilies.

Midges, gnats and mosquitoes

These lay their eggs in water, where the larvae and pupae live until developing the mature adult form. One midge lays eggs on the leaves of plants such as *Aponogeton distachyus* (water hawthorn) and nymphaea (water lilies). The slender, transparent larvae burrow in the leaf tissues, eventually leaving a mere skeleton of ribs – a heavy infestation can badly damage or even kill miniature lilies such as *Nymphaea pygmaea helvola*. Remove and destroy affected leaves, or alternatively lift the plant and immerse it for an hour in a bucket of insecticide of the kind used for spraying aphids. The plant must be rinsed well before replanting.

Apply the same treatment to any other lilies if the roots have been invaded by the 13mm ($\frac{1}{2}$in) long, bright red larvae (known as bloodworms) of another type of midge. The best and first line of defence against these airborne nuisances is a shoal of small golden orfe, always on the alert for any insect that so much as touches the water surface.

Beetles

Even the completely aquatic types of beetle fly much more readily than is generally realized, and every new pond is soon colonized by many species. Most are small and entirely harmless, and the large, fish-killing great diving beetle, *Dytiscus marginalis*, is the only aquatic one that need cause concern. Watch out for it especially in early – mid summer (May – June).

Two other beetles, both living not in the water but on water plants, may turn up. One is a dull brown, ladybird-sized creature, *Galeruca nymphaea* (water lily beetle). Both this and the dingy, yellow-bellied larva cut channels in the upper surface of lily leaves, reducing them eventually to a black pulp. The beetle and its larva are common where lilies are grown in quantity, but fortunately do not turn up very often in small ponds. Destruction of affected leaves, complete with beetles, larvae and yellow egg clusters, soon eliminates them.

The other pond-dwelling beetle that keeps its feet dry belongs to a group known, because of its metallic, gleaming red, green or bronze colouring, as the water jewels. It feeds on plant leaves, but the damage is too slight to justify any

measures against these beautiful insects.

Water boatmen

Strictly speaking, these are bugs with sucking mouth parts, but to the layman they are simply another kind of beetle. They are recognized easily from their habit of swimming upside down with strong beats of a pair of oar-like legs, and their characteristic resting attitude at the surface, upside down, with the end of the body and the 'oar' tips just touching the surface film. Though not much more than 13mm ($\frac{1}{2}$ in) long, they are capable of killing small fish, and should be netted out and disposed of.

Whirligigs

These can dive below the surface but are usually seen in groups dashing about in frenzied gyrations on the surface, their tiny, blue-black bodies gleaming in the sunlight. They are harmless.

Water skaters and springtails

Among dwellers on top of the surface film are water skaters, with long-legged, slender bodies of maybe 2–3cm (1 in) length, and several species of springtails, some so small that they look like particles of soot. Both may appear in large numbers at times, but need cause no alarm since they are merely scavengers of dead insects and other small debris that settles on the surface of the pond.

Leeches

These are present in most ponds, although they live in obscurity in the mud, their existence only suspected when empty snail shells are found. The true fish-leech has a body with alternate dark- and light-coloured bands, and is very rare. Dark olive-brown leeches can attack fish if their normal prey – snails, tadpoles and insect larvae – runs short.

If you suspect that your pond has an excessive leech population you should treat it with Sterazin P, preferably more than once in the course of the summer to ensure that any young leeches emerging from eggs after the first treatment are completely eliminated. However, this treatment is not advisable if the pond contains any orfe, when trappings must be resorted to instead. The trap consists merely of a small tin (such as might have contained cat food) with three or four 7mm ($\frac{1}{4}$ in) holes in the sides, near the base. This is baited with a piece of raw meat or liver and placed on the bottom of the pond overnight. If there are leeches present most of them will be found attached to the bait when the tin is lifted out in the morning. The best way to dispose of them is to drop them in boiling water. Repeat the process at intervals until there are no further catches.

In Britain, incidentally, leeches – though thoroughly repellent to many

Below: this water snail is probably feeding on algae attached to the water-milfoil. Below far left: medicinal leech (Hirudo medicinalis) *is the largest British leech measuring up to 12cm ($4\frac{1}{2}$ in). Below left: the long legs of the adult pond skater enable it to glide at speed across the surface of the water. Below centre: mass of harmless whirlygig beetles. Bottom: clusters of scavenging springtails on pond surface.*

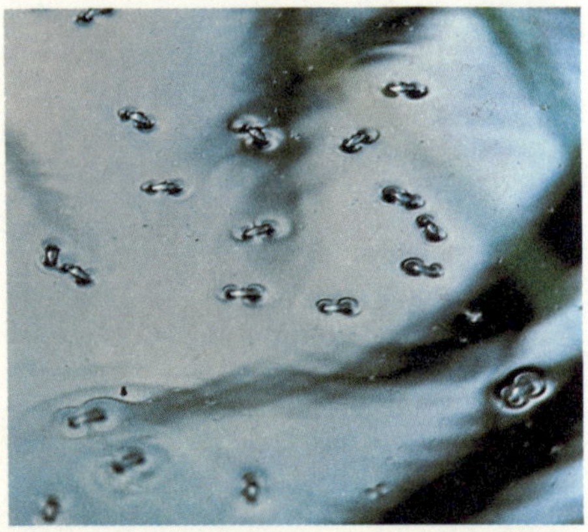

people – are not harmful, since there is no indigenous species that is capable of piercing the human skin.

China mark moths

It seems unlikely that oval holes 2–3cm (1 in) long in lily leaves could be caused by a frail-looking, black-and-white moth that flutters weakly around the pond in the dusk of midsummer evenings. In fact, the holes are the work of its caterpillar, that will probably be found beneath the leaf, snug in a silk-lined home formed between the cut-out oval and the leaf's underside.

Caterpillars may be found moving about the pond wearing a case formed by two oval pieces of lily leaf. The damage to the leaves is seldom sufficient to weaken the plant, and stern countermeasures are not often called for. If there is a plague of them the only action possible is to examine all lily leaves and pick off the caterpillars by hand.

Right: the great pond snail, as its name suggests, is one of the largest freshwater snails, reaching up to 6cm (2½ in) in shell height. Here, a great ram's horn snail is hitching a ride on its back. Below: the wandering snail, Britain's most common species, is very variable in appearance.

Planarian flatworms

An examination of lily leaves could also reveal the flat, oval, dark brown, leathery-looking egg cocoons of leeches, that are best destroyed, as well as some harmless creatures that are often confused with leeches. The last are planarian flatworms, and they are perhaps 13mm (½in) or so in length, and usually black, but sometimes grey or even white. They glide, whereas most leeches move by looping rather like geometer caterpillars. Flatworms are harmless and can be ignored.

Snails

You may notice some blobs of jelly on the underside of lily leaves. If these are roundish, flat, and amber in colour, they will be the egg clusters of the harmless black ramshorn snail. Sausage-shaped blobs, on the other hand, are often assumed to be some sort of slug, but in fact are the egg clusters of a snail called *Limnaea stagnalis*. Removing the clusters is one of the easiest ways of controlling this undesirable plant-destroyer.

Other visitors

The activities of frogs, toads and newts seldom constitute more than a mild, temporary nuisance, and their arrival cannot be prevented anyway, while dragonflies are entirely harmless and should be enjoyed for their beauty.

A-Z PESTS AND DISEASES

Adelgids Aphids belonging to the family ADELGIDAE that attack coniferous trees, causing stunting and premature leaf-fall; some cause galls, others secrete a white, waxy covering. Also known as conifer gall-lice. (See also Aphids).

Opposite: a thriving front garden. Below: galls on a conifer caused by the presence of adelgids. Bottom: freshwater algae should be cleared from pools.

Algae A large class of primitive plants, ranging from the comparatively complex seaweeds to the flannel or blanketweed of pools, and the green slime on wet paths, tiles and pots, to the green 'powder' seen on wooden fence posts and tree trunks. Their presence on soil and pots generally denotes excess moisture and sour conditions. Flannelweed is a nuisance in newly-made pools, particularly shallow ones that warm up quickly. Once the pool has matured with the addition of water plants, fish and pond snails, flannelweed usually dies out naturally. During its worst phase, however, it is best pulled out regularly with a rake. Provided a tree is healthy and well cared for, a small amount of algae on the trunk will do no harm. Proprietary substances are available to prevent paths and pots getting green and slimy but are not always totally successful.

American gooseberry mildew (*Sphaerotheca mors-uvae*) This shows first as thick, white, powdery patches on leaves and fruit while in the final phase there is a brownish, felty covering on the berries. It is essential to stop this fungus early, as soon as you see the first white patches on the young leaves and shoots. Apply a systemic fungicide at once and repeat at 10–14 day intervals if necessary.

Anthracnose A fungus disease causing dark, oval or rounded, depressed areas in plant tissues. Bean anthracnose attacks stems and pods of dwarf french and runner beans, while grapevine a. causes sunken areas in the berries and spots or holes in the leaves. In the latter case cut out all infected growth and spray with strong lime sulphur in winter. Beans should be grown in a drier, warmer site. Disease is seed-transmitted so always use fresh seed. Anthracnose of willows is caused by the fungus *Marssonina salicola*. It produces red-brown spotting on the leaves, pale brown lesions on the stems and dieback of their tips. In wet seasons damage can be severe, particularly on weeping willows which are prevented from making new, pendent stems. Control is difficult, especially on large trees. Spray with Bordeaux mixture just before the buds break in early spring and repeat at periods of three weeks until July avoiding spells of hot weather.

Ants Communal insects, members of *Hymenoptera,* to which bees and wasps also belong. They do limited damage to plants, mainly to flowers in a search for nectar. Their most troublesome habits are protecting and distributing aphids, which they milk like cows for their sweet

Below: black garden ants, swarming.

Left: woolly aphids hidden within the fluffy white 'wool' – a wax-like substance secreted from the cornicles. Far left, top: an aphid giving birth to live offspring. All the aphids found in summer are female and capable of giving birth, without being fertilized, to several offspring in one day. Top centre: ladybirds, like this 7-spot, and their larvae, sometimes consume as many as 100 aphids in a single day.
Bottom centre: rose shoot with adult and young aphids. Bottom: black bean aphids are also known as black blight and black fly. In summer their host-plant is broad bean, sugar beet, spinach and docks.

excretions, and digging much-branched tunnel nests under the roots of plants, that then may die of drought as all water rapidly drains away. Control by applying HCH (BHC) or one of the virus ant-killers.

Aphids Green- or blackflies, plant lice; small, softbodied insects, members of the order *Hemiptera* (true bugs), family APHIDIDAE, that suck sap, weakening the plant and causing curling or crippling of stems, leaves, flowers; some also live on roots. Apart from the direct damage, aphids transmit virus diseases from plant to plant. In addition, they secrete a sweet, sticky fluid beloved by ants, wasps and some butterflies (see Ants entry). This fluid can fall like fine rain when a large shrub or tree – for example, a lime tree – is infested, and forms a coating on leaves that is soon colonized by sooty moulds, creating a blackish, unsightly appearance. The life cycle of many aphid species is surprisingly complex. Some of the commonest overwinter in the egg stage on a shrub or tree (the primary host plant), eg blackfly on spindle. In spring the eggs hatch and the young aphids soon mature into 'stem mothers' that give rise to a continuous succession of living young by virgin birth (parthenogenesis). In late spring or summer, winged individuals develop that fly off to the secondary or summer host plants, usually annuals and perennials, eg beans, docks etc, and these produce further generations of wingless aphids. In early autumn a winged generation again arises that flies back to the primary host plants and produces more wingless females plus males, the only time in the life cycle that the latter occur. After mating, overwintering eggs are laid and the adults die off. Some aphids bypass this complete cycle and reproduce parthenogenetically the whole year round, overwintering in densely leaved plants or sheltered corners; these can be very troublesome in greenhouses or inside the home, even in winter.

Most of the commoner aphids are shades of green, yellow, brown, black, pink or grey. The grey colour is due to a whitish secretion and is characteristic of the cabbage aphid, the woolly aphid or American blight of apples, and many adelgids, very closely allied insects in the family ADELGIDAE. The adelgids attack only conifer trees and some are serious pests. Both aphids and adelgids have members that live in galls or blister-like swellings, eg currant aphid causes red blisters on the leaves, poplar aphid produces galls on leaf-stalks, and spruce adelgid forms 'pineapple' or 'pseudo-cone' galls by attacking all the leaf bases of the young shoot.

Aphids have many natural enemies, notably ladybirds, lacewing fly and hoverfly larvae, and also birds such as tits. In gardens and especially under glass these predators are often not able to keep aphid populations down below pest level and spraying must then be resorted to, using one of the many proprietary formulations.

Apple Sawfly, see Sawflies.

Apple Sucker (*Psylla mali*) A tiny insect in the family PSYLLIDAE and order *Hemiptera* (true bugs) not unlike a winged aphid when mature, but wingless and crab-like when young. It overwinters as eggs on spurs and twigs, the young emerging in spring and entering expanding buds, sucking sap and causing flower-buds to shrivel and leaves to wrinkle. Not usually a severe pest and easily controlled by tar-oil winter wash, HCH or malathion.

Asparagus beetle (*Crioceris asparagi*) The main pest of asparagus. The grey larvae of this little creature are particularly destructive in their attacks on the stem and fern during late summer and early autumn (July and August). Examine the ferns from time to time and, if you find the pests, treat with derris dust. A second application, 10–14 days later, will kill any grubs that have emerged from the eggs since the first dusting.

Asparagus fly (*Platyparea poeciloptera*) Insect that lays her eggs in late spring and early summer (April and May) on the young shoots. The yellowish-white maggots tunnel into the shoots, causing them to wilt. Cut out all affected shoots and burn them. Fortunately this pest is not so common as the beetle.

Asparagus rust (*Puccinia asparagi*) An uncommon fungus disease, that appears on the stems and foliage of the plants from late summer (July) onwards. This takes the form of small reddish pustules that turn darker as the season advances. Dusting the foliage with flowers of sulphur will help to keep the fungus at bay.

Bacteria Minute, single-celled plants generally lacking chlorophyll and multiplying by simple division (binary fission). There are three principal groups based upon their shape: **1** *coccus* (spherical). **2** *bacillus* or *bacterium* (rod-shaped). **3** *spirillium, spirochaete, vibrio* (spiral forms). In addition, the bacteria in these groupings may live in chains, or groups known as packets. The life-cycles of bacteria are varied but they are mainly parasites (on living plant and animal tissue) or saprophytes (living on dead plant and animal tissue). Saprophytes are important members of the soil fauna, breaking down the carbohydrates of organic matter into humus. Of particular interest are the nitrogen-fixing bacteria that live in partnership mainly with leguminous (pea family) plants. Known as *Rhizobium*, these bacteria enter root-hairs and their irritation causes the plant tissue to form tiny galls called nodules. The bacteria live within these, synthesizing organic nitrogen from the air and using sugars from the plant as an energy source. The plant can utilize the organic nitrogen and thus most members of the pea family can grow healthily in nitrogen-deficient soils. When the plant dies the remaining nodule nitrogen is released into the soil. Some bacteria are free-living, synthesizing carbohydrates from carbon dioxide and water like higher plants, but in the absence of chlorophyll they obtain energy from the oxidation of such substances as iron and sulphuretted hydrogen. The important nitrifying bacteria oxidize nitrates and ammonium salts to nitrates, in each case making nitrogen suitable for absorption by the roots of higher plants. For important diseases of higher plants caused by parasitic bacteria, see Crown gall, Gladiolus scab, Potato blackleg, Soft rot.

Barberry rust, *see* Rust fungus.

Bark Beetles Small beetles allied to the weevils and classified in the family SCOLYTIDAE. They can be divided into two main groups: those that live in the bark alone, and the wood-borers (also known as shot-hole borers or ambrosia beetles) that tunnel into the wood. The larvae (grubs) of the latter group live on fungi that inhabit the tunnels; elm bark beetle is a good example, the fungus it helps to spread being the deadly Dutch elm disease. In general, however, these tiny beetles attack trees already weakened by old age, diseases, or such factors as waterlogging, or prolonged drought. Young, healthy trees are seldom attacked. In large trees the beetles are difficult to control unless there is access to aerial spraying facilities or inoculation equipment. Limited success is achieved by drenching the ground with a systemic insecticide, but it is seldom worth the trouble and expense.

Barren Used mainly to describe plants grown for their fruit, but which persistently fail to produce a crop. These are frequently individual specimens that are either self-sterile and need a pollinator, eg sweet cherry, or are the male plants of a dioecious species, eg holly, willow. Alternatively, the plant may be a completely sterile hybrid or mutant.

Bees Members of the insect order *Hymenoptera*, some species of which live socially (honey bee) and some solitarily (eg mining and leaf-cutter bees, the females alone making a nest and stocking it with food, but dying before the next generation emerges). Honey bees (*Apis*), bumble bees (*Bombus*), and most of the solitary bees are useful pollinators in the garden, particularly of fruit blossom. However, some bumble bees bypass these potentially useful activities by biting holes in the bases of the longer-tubed flowers to get at the deep-seated nectar. Leaf-cutting bees (*Megachile*) can be a nuisance, cutting neat circles and ovals from leaves of roses and other plants with which to make their nests. Damage is rarely severe and little can be done to prevent it except trying to trace the bee to its nest and destroying that.

Beetles Members of the *Coleoptera*, the largest order of insects and of the entire animal kingdom, containing some 250,000 known species. Varying from minute to very large, they are mainly characterized by having two, rigid, close-fitting upper or outer wings lying side by

Above left: larvae of the bark beetle Scolytus, *in elm wood. Left: beetle-breeding galleries in elm bark. In spring the beetles fly to new trees, carrying the fungus with them.*

Above: ground beetle, a beneficial insect rather than a pest. Right: big bud on blackcurrant is caused by a microscopic mite that attacks the bud's inside, causing an abnormal enlargement.

side along the back of the body. Several species are pests, notably bark beetle, blossom weevil, flea beetle, pea and bean, pineshoot, poplar, raspberry, seed and vine weevils, water-lily beetle, qv. A number of beetles are beneficial, eg ladybirds and ground-beetles.

Beetroot viruses Two fairly common virus diseases infect beetroot. Mosaic causes yellow flecking or mottling and veining of the leaves. Leaf distortion also occurs, mainly as a curling back of the margins and tips. If severely attacked the whole plant is stunted. In the case of the other virus, known as beet yellows or mild yellowing, the leaves become thickened, dry and brittle with a flush of red and yellow. Sometimes there are also brown spots between the veins. These viruses are spread by aphids and eliminating the aphids by regular spraying goes a good way towards prevention. This must be reinforced by a regular attention to weeding, as certain weeds (notably docks, goosefoots and fat hen) harbour the virus organisms and act as reservoirs of infection.

Big bud Pest of blackcurrants caused by the microscopic mite *Eriophyes ribis* (*Phytoptus r.*) that attacks the bud's inside, bringing about an abnormal enlargement or galled condition. Infected buds never develop normally and heavily-attacked bushes crop poorly and may die. The mites leave the buds in early summer and move to the newly-forming buds on young stems. At this time a spraying with lime sulphur will kill many. Badly infected bushes are best destroyed or individual stems removed and burnt in winter, followed later by spraying.

The only variety of blackcurrant in present cultivation that has some degree of immunity to gall mites is Seabrook's Black. It is not completely immune, but may go for several years without an infestation.

Birds Often among the attractions of gardens; but a few are pests and need controlling by one means or another. Most damage is done by the bullfinch, house sparrow, starling, blue tit, wood pigeon and blackbird. Chemical repellents are largely unreliable; sometimes they work well enough for short periods, but often they seem useless. Scaring devices also have a limited effect. Scarecrows sometimes work if moved about every few days. Recorded distress calls of the birds themselves are sometimes very effective as are the explosive scarers. The latter are generally too noisy for the home garden. Glittering foil strips are moderately effective but on still days birds ignore them. Black cotton criss-crossed over seed beds and crocus and polyanthus flowers is highly effective, but birds can get caught by their feet and die of starvation. For this reason, thin cotton thread, which is easily broken, must be used. Nylon thread is too strong. Cages or "hats" of chicken wire are easily made and can quickly be placed over a special plant under attack, eg any small grey-leaved species being shredded by starlings for nesting material. If fruit is to be protected then netting and, ideally, a properly constructed cage is the only answer.

Below: the goldfinch should not be treated as a pest. In autumn they feed on the seeds of various weeds.

Bitterpit Condition of apple fruits, recognized as small, dark, often somewhat sunken spots, just under the skin or deeper. It is not a disease, but is due to a lack of calcium. If the soil is known to be acid, an annual dressing of lime should be applied in autumn at not less than 60g per sq m (2 oz per sq yd).

Blackberry mite (*Phytoptus essigii*) A condition that frequently mystifies gardeners, particularly when the season is ideal for ripening, is failure of the berries to ripen fully. Many of the drupels (the small globules of which the berries are composed, and that contain the seeds) remain red. Himalaya is probably the most widely affected. This trouble is caused by the blackberry mite, sometimes called red berry mite, a microscopic species that feeds on the berries, preventing the drupels from ripening, and often causing distortion. Complete control is difficult to achieve but the mites can be substantially reduced by burning canes carrying infested berries immediately after harvest, and following this up next season with a spray of lime sulphur in early summer (mid May) at 500ml to 10 litres (1pt to 2½ gal) water; or a solution of wettable sulphur in water at 50g to 10 litres (2oz per 2½ gal) water just before flowering. Lime sulphur may cause some leaf scorch, but this is not usually enough to do serious damage. Wettable sulphur is not the same as sulphur dust; the latter is not formulated for use as a spray and should not be used as such.

Above: black spot on a rose. Right: a potato crop infected with blight, Phytophthora infestans. *In cool, moist weather this fungus can wipe out huge areas of the crop.*

Black Leg Disease caused by several fungi and bacteria, that produces a basal black rot of cuttings, particularly geraniums (*Pelargonium*) and succulents. The use of sterilized compost and clean water, and avoiding overwatering, usually eliminates the disease.

Black Spot (*Diplocarpon rosae*) Disease of roses that causes blackish blotches on the leaves and later, premature leaf-fall. Some roses are more susceptible than others, notably the heavily-pruned Hybrid Tea and Floribunda groups. To control, spray at fortnightly intervals from spring to autumn with captan or maneb. The disease overwinters on fallen leaves, so initially rake up and burn all infected leaves. Keep bushes vigorous and healthy by mulching and feeding (foliar feeds are good) as the disease will be much more severe on weakly-growing bushes.

Bleeding Long-term exudation of sap after pruning or damage to stems. Although not considered desirable, it does not appear to be injurious. Plants prone to bleeding, eg grape vine, many deciduous trees etc, should be pruned in summer or autumn soon after leaf-fall.

Blight General name for several pests and diseases that wither, brown or defoliate plants in a rapid, sometimes spectacular way. Heavy infestations of black fly and other aphids are also sometimes called blight. Potato blight is caused by the fungus *Phytophthora infestans*, which turns leaves brown and withered, and can spread quickly in humid, still weather in summer. Spores from the leaves can also be washed into the soil, where they attack the young tubers, which later brown and rot. Control can be effected by spraying with maneb, zineb or Bordeaux mixture at 10–14 day intervals during the summer or as soon as the first signs are recognized – usually yellow patches on the leaves that spread and turn brown. Outdoor tomatoes are also attacked in the same way,

Blind, Blindness Terms used to describe young plants that reach a certain stage of growth then stop and get no further, owing to the death or non-functioning of the growing point; cabbages, cauliflowers and other brassicas often provide examples. The cause may be genetic, or due to hormone sprays or insect damage. In bulbous plants, blindness is failure to develop flowers, generally caused by lack of water when the young buds are expanding. Bulbs in bowls kept at too high temperatures are very prone to this.

Blossom End Rot Disorder of tomatoes, showing as circular brown patches around the blossom end of the fruit, which later becomes sunken and rotten. It is not a disease, but caused by lack of calcium. If the soil is known to be acid, apply a dressing of lime at 60g per sq m (2 oz per sq yd) at planting time.

Blossom Wilt *see* Brown Rot.

Blotchy Ripening Disorder of tomatoes showing as irregular patches on ripe fruit. It appears to be caused by lack of potash or nitrogen often combined with over-high greenhouse temperatures. Applying a balanced fertilizer before planting and during growth, plus good ventilation once the temperature is over 21°C (70°F), will ensure that this trouble does not happen.

Blue mould rot This is commonly seen on bulbs, corms and tubers in store. It is usually first recognised as a blue-white or blue-grey mould. This is the fruiting stage of the *Penicillium* species responsible. Earlier, browning or reddish lesions would have been seen particularly on the sides of crocuses, gladioli, tigridias, etc. The mould spreads rapidly in store and is often worse on bulbs which do not like being kept out of the ground, eg lilies, bluebells and summer hyacinth. Planting should therefore be carried out as soon as possible. Severely attacked bulbs and corms must be destroyed. Less severely damaged ones should be dipped in benomyl solution for at least 15–30 minutes before planting.

Bolting When vegetable crops, eg radish, turnip, beetroot etc send up flowering stems prematurely. It usually happens after a severe check to growth such as drought or lack of nitrogen. In sugar beet, the tendency to bolt has a genetic factor and seed should never be saved from any bolter.

Boron Micronutrient or trace element essential for the process of cell division. Basically, deficiency results in a crippling of developing tissues and death of growing points, giving rise to several 'diseases'

Below: tomatoes with blossom end rot. This is not a disease, but is caused by lack of calcium.

(physiological disorders), eg crown rot and canker of beet, curd browning of cauliflowers, cracked stem or brown crack of celery, brown heart of turnip and swede, and drought spot and corky core of apple. Sweet corn fails to develop cobs and has whitish streaks in the leaves. Remedy by applying borax at 1·5g per sq m (¼ oz per 6 sq yd) of soil, preferably first mixing with dry sand to make sure of even dispersal.

Botrytis Genus of fungi, several species of which are important diseases of familiar fruit, vegetables and flowers. They attack living, damaged and dead tissues of a wide range of plants. The spore-bearing hyphae grow densely, producing a grey-white mould. Common grey mould (*B. cinerea*) is most prevalent in cool, humid weather, attacking soft shoots and leaves, particularly in unheated frames and greenhouses in winter. It can be serious on immature strawberry fruit, which quickly browns and rots. Remove all diseased tissue as soon as seen and dust with captan, or spray with thiram, zineb or dichlofluanid. See also Gooseberry dieback, Lily disease. Peony blight and Tulip fire.

Bracket Fungi General term for the fruiting (spore-bearing) bodies of a group of fungi in the class BASIDIOMYCETES. They occur on living or dead wood, eg trunks and branches, and appear as half-moon shaped or flange-like objects projecting at right-angles to their support. Most are shades of brown and grey above, paler beneath. On a living tree trunk their presence usually means the tree is so badly infected that its days are numbered. If they appear on a branch only, that branch should be severed flush with the trunk and the wound covered with a bituminous paint or one of the proprietary substances now available. As a preventative, always treat wounds in this way and if possible do the pruning in summer. See Fungi.

Brown core Attacks polyanthus and primula roots, and the plants then become weak and sickly. Burn all affected plants and grow no others of the family on that ground for several years.

Brown Heart Physiological disorder of turnips, swedes and beetroot, caused through lack of the trace element boron (qv). It shows as a browning and withering of the central leaves, and brownish or greyish areas within the root that cause bitterness. The remedy is to apply borax at 30g per 15 sq m (1 oz per 15 sq yd), mixing with dry sand first to get an even distribution.

Brown Rot Disease of fruit, mainly apples, but sometimes pears, plums, cherries and peaches, caused by the fungus *Sclerotinia fructigena*. It produces a soft, brown, rapidly spreading rot, either in store or while the fruit is still on the tree. In the latter case the fruit later dries and withers, becoming 'mummied' or mummified, bearing concentric rings of whitish or yellowish sporing pustules. All infected fruit should be destroyed as soon as possible, that on the tree being removed with part of the spur which also frequently becomes infected. Make sure that fruit put in store is free of bruises or other damage, and look it over regularly for signs of rot. Wrapping individual fruits, or storing them in moulded trays designed to keep them separate will prevent rot spreading. Brown rot disease is also responsible for the conditions known as blossom wilt, spur blight and wither tip. At first, flowers and/or young leaves wilt either on spurs or short tips, usually with small cankers or brown lesions just below the lowest withered leaf. Later, there is dieback of larger stems. Cut out all affected twigs as soon as they appear. However, it is far better to prevent severe infection by spraying with Bordeaux Mixture or liquid copper fungicide just pre-flower. Ornamental plums and cherries can also suffer from blossom wilt and spur blight.

Right: brown rot on apples. Below: a species of bracket fungus Ganoderma *attacking a beech tree.*

Bryobia *see* Spider mite.

Bud-drop General term covering the premature falling of flower-buds on a wide variety of plants. Dryness at the roots, sudden changes of temperature (under glass), overwatering and starvation are the primary causes. Making sure these cultural errors do not occur will ensure freedom from bud-drop. Susceptible plants include begonia, fuchsia, sweet pea, tomato, especially when pot-grown.

Bulb Scale Mite (*Tarsonemus laticeps*) Microscopic, colourless or pinkish creature $\frac{1}{10}$mm ($\frac{1}{250}$ in) long, living in large colonies between the scales of bulbs, mainly those of narcissi and hippeastrums (amaryllis). Apart from weakening of the bulbs, visible signs of damage are rusty-brown or red areas and streaks on the leaves and flowers, plus some crippling and distortion. The cure is to place the bulbs when dormant in water at a constant temperature of 43·5°C (110°F) for one hour. This requires an accurate thermometer and frequent small injections of warm water, well stirred in, to maintain the constant temperature, unless there is access to thermostatically-controlled commercial or laboratory equipment. Bulbs damaged by insects and other creatures are sometimes attacked by bulb mite (*Rhizoglyhus echinopus*), a glossy, rounded, yellow-white creature 1mm ($\frac{1}{25}$in) long and just visible to the naked eye. These mites breed rapidly and kill the bulb. Slightly infected bulbs can be given warm-water treatment, three hours at 43·5°C (110°F), but generally they are best destroyed by burning.

Cabbage Butterflies Gardeners' name for the large white (*Pieris brassica*) and small white (*P. rapae*) butterflies, common insects around brassicas in summer. They are a conspicuous white with black-tipped fore-wings, those of the female also having 2 central black spots. Both species lay eggs on cabbages and other members of the CRUCIFERAE family, also garden nasturtiums (*Tropaeolum*). The caterpillars (larvae) of the large white are brindled black and yellow and are often found in large numbers on the surface of cabbage leaves, reducing them to a skeleton of veins. Those of the small white are a soft, velvety green, living solitarily on leaf undersides, often around the hearts. They are easily controlled by spraying with derris or several other proprietary insecticides, used to makers' instructions. In addition, the tiny, spindle-shaped, yellow eggs usually laid on leaf undersides may be looked for and squashed between the fingers.

Cabbage-root fly (*Delia brassicae*) The transplanting period is the time when precautions should be taken against this pest that lays its eggs against the stems of the plants. The maggots that hatch from the eggs burrow into the soil and attack the stems below soil level. Affected plants wilt in sunshine and will eventually collapse. It is always advisable to give the ground a routine dressing of bromophos or diazinon to prevent this pest. As an alternative method, mix some powder in water to form a paste, and then dip the roots and stems in the paste as you are transplanting.

If, in spite of this treatment (or due to lack of it), you find that cabbage-root fly has taken hold do not write the crop off. If the attack is not too severe you can encourage the plants to overcome it by forming new roots. They will do this if earth is drawn up under the lower leaves so that the stems are covered. Providing that you never allow them to dry out, these new roots will be enough to carry the crop through.

Below: large cabbage white butterfly caterpillars on brassicas. Bottom: cabbage-root fly larvae.

Calcium Essential element for the life of all plants, even those classified as calcifuge, but generally needed in very small amounts. Calcium is tied up with the movement of carbohydrates in the plant, neutralizes acids and aids in the entry of such essential plant foods as nitrates, phosphates and sulphates, with which it combines. Calcium does not occur in a pure state but combines with other substances, mainly carbonic acid, to form chalk, limestone, marble, etc. It is also a main constituent of bones as calcium phosphate, and shells and coral as calcium carbonate. Deficiency of lime, a generally rare occurrence, can show as weak growth from shoot tips, poor root action, wilting of shoots, leaf and flower-stalks, poor tuber formation, particularly in potatoes. See also Blossom end rot and Bitterpit.

Cane Blight (*Leptosphaeria coniothyrium*) Disease mainly of raspberries, particularly the cultivars Lloyd George and Norfolk Giant. It attacks the bases of canes, causing a cracking of the stem accompanied by tiny, black, spherical fruiting bodies, and wilting of the foliage above. Infected canes must be cut out well below ground level and the plants sprayed with copper or Bordeaux mixture.

Cane Spot (*Elsinoe veneta*) Disease of raspberry, loganberry and the various hybrid berries, attacking the canes and causing purplish spots that later become sunken, the surrounding stem showing cracks. The leaves may show small, circular, white-centred, dark-edged spots. Infected fruit may be misshapen. The plant is weakened and fruit poorly. Remove and destroy badly-spotted canes and spray with a 5 per cent lime sulphur, copper or thiram, according to makers' instructions, just as the buds break in spring.

Canker General term for wounds in the stems of woody plants that do not heal

Above: canker (Nectria galligena) *attack on an apple tree, recognizable by the ridge of callous tissue surrounding the cut which has failed to heal properly. Right: the capsid bug* Mirus striatus *is omniverous, feeding on aphids, insect eggs and larvae, as well as the young parts of trees which can cause considerable damage to the whole tree.*

properly. They are usually recognized as sunken areas often deeply-cracked, surrounded by a ridge of callus tissue. They can spread around a stem, girdling it and killing the growth beyond. The primary injury may be a wound caused by insects, mammals or man, eg the chafing of a loose stake-tie followed by the attack of one of several fungi. The most important of these is apple canker (*Nectria galligena*), attacking apple, pear, beech, ash, poplar and sorbus. Small infected stems or spurs and almost girdled larger ones should be cut out well below the canker area, the stump being painted over with white lead or a proprietary canker paint. On larger branches that are less than half girdled cut out the canker area with a sharp knife or chisel until clean white wood is reached, then treat as already stated. If cankers are frequent, spray the whole tree with a copper fungicide or Bordeaux mixture as soon as the fruit is picked and before leaf-fall.

Capsid Bugs Large group of sucking insects, members of the order *Hemiptera* (true bugs) and family MIRIDAE (CAPSIDAE). They are small, flattened, green or brown insects about 6mm (¼ in) long and rather like beetles but with 'wing covers' (forewings) having transparent tips. A wide range of plants are attacked, particularly trees and shrubs; capsid bugs have a preference for sucking soft young flower-buds, fruit, shoot tips and leaves, which later results in perforated or tattered leaves and distorted stems, flowers and fruit. The most damaging species are: the tarnished plant or bishop bug (*Lygus pratensis*), yellow-green, mottled red-brown, feeding mainly on annuals and perennial plants, including weeds such as dock and groundsel, also dahlia, chrysanthemum, zinnia etc; common green capsid (*Lygus pabulinus*), bright green, on currants, gooseberry and other fruit, also on many other trees, shrubs and perennials; apple capsid (*Plesiocoris rugicollis*), green, often on apple, currants, gooseberry, willow—sometimes a serious pest of the apple, causing malformed fruit. The last two capsids overwinter as eggs on the host trees or shrubs, the bishop bug as adults among old weed stems and rough herbage. The eggs of the tree and shrub species can be killed by tar oil and DNOC winter wash-sprays, the active stages of all by HCH (BHC), used according to makers' instructions. Not all capsid bugs are harmful: the black-kneed capsid (*Blepharidopterus angulatus*), much like a common green capsid but with black knee joints, feeds largely on fruit tree red spider mites, often a serious pest of apples.

Carnation fly Also known as carnation leaf-miner and scientifically as *Delia cardui*, this pest confines its activities to carnations, pinks, sweet williams and other members of the genus *Dianthus*. Eggs are laid in September and the whitish larvae tunnel along the middle of the leaves and into stem tips. Attacked leaves and stems die. Feeding takes place in autumn and winter, and the adult, rather like a small house fly emerges in June. Control can be effected by spraying with dimethoate or HCH as soon as the mines are seen.

Carnation viruses Several virus diseases affect carnations and other sorts of *Dianthus*, two of which are widespread in Britain. Carnation mottle reduces vigour and usually produces a pale yellow mottling, sometimes in the form of diffuse ring-marks. It is spread by handling and probably by sucking insects. Ring spot virus often accompanies mottle. It shows as yellow rings and ring spots some of which turn brown (necrosis). There is also a bending, buckling or lateral distortion of the leaves. The plant as a whole is stunted and lacks vigour and the flowers are small, pale and badly shaped. Less common is carnation vein mottle seen locally on sweet williams. Pale yellowish mottling appears on the leaves and fewer flowers are produced, their colours often broken (irregular segments of another colour break up the usual pattern). This virus is spread by aphids. Infected plants should be destroyed and the remainder kept regularly sprayed against aphids and other sucking insects. Most specialist nurserymen sell virus-free stocks of standard cultivars and seed raised plants are automatically free if kept clean of pests.

Carrot fly (*Psila rosae*) Tiny fly with a greenish-black body about 6mm (¼ in) long. It lays eggs in the soil near young carrot plants and the tiny, colourless to whitish larvae (maggots) tunnel into the roots. Severe attacks produce stunted plants that wilt in dry or warm weather

Below: carrot fly larvae (maggots) tunnelling into a carrot root.

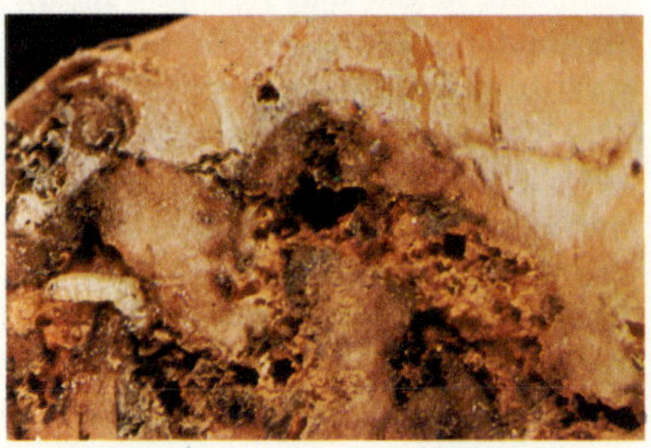

Left: this garden carpet caterpillar (Xanthorhoe fluctuata) *is moving with the characteristic looping motion across a sprout leaf, a common food source. Above: rose chafer* (Cetonia aurata).

and show yellow or reddish leaves; the roots are largely uneatable. There are two broods a year, eggs being laid in early and late summer. Crops sown early outside – especially under cloches – and a main crop sown mid to late summer are likely to be free of this pest. The odour of crushed leaves attracts the female flies, so care must be taken when thinning and this is best done in the cool of early morning or evening. Where attacks are known to be troublesome, BHC (HCH) dust may be applied to the soil at sowing time or at first thinning, but this can sometimes give the carrots an earthy taint. Alternatively, the flies can be largely deterred by dusting the soil with 3–4 applications of powdered or flaked naphthalene, commencing immediately after the first thinning.

Caterpillars General name for juvenile or larval stage of butterflies and moths, members of the insect order *Lepidoptera*. They are soft, cylindrical creatures having hard, rounded heads furnished with vertical jaws. The typical caterpillar, eg that of the large white cabbage butterfly, has three pairs of small, true legs close to the head and five pairs of false or pro-legs (sucker feet), four in the middle and 1 pair at the 'tail' end. Exceptions to this are the loopers or geometers, caterpillars of a large group of moths in the family GEOMETRIDAE that have only two pairs of pro-legs at the end of the body, and the semi-loopers (PLUSIIDAE) with three pairs only. The larvae of sawflies much resemble, and are confused with, those of butterflies and moths but always have six pairs of pro-legs. Caterpillars may be smooth or hairy and are generally in shades of green or brown with or without a pattern of contrasting colour, eg lackey moth. They feed mainly on leaves and flowers, some species also eating fruit, seed, roots and wood (see Codling moth). In general, all the leaf-feeders are easily dealt with by hand-picking or spraying with derris, HCH (BHC), malathion, trichlorphon, or one of the many proprietary formulations.

Celery fly (*Philophylla heraclei*) Also known as celery leaf-miner, this member of the insect order *Diptera* (true flies) is a common pest of celery and parsnip. The legless white larvae (maggots) tunnel within the leaf tissue causing large, pale, blister-like patches on the leaflets that finally turn brownish and wither. The adult fly has a wing span of 10–12mm ($\frac{2}{5}$–$\frac{1}{2}$ in), each wing having a striking pattern of reddish to blackish brown bands. The eyes are deep green. There are two generations a year, early summer and early autumn. Severely attacked plants lose vigour and grow poorly. Keep a watch for the first signs of mining, particularly in mid-summer and mid-autumn. If the attack is a light one, regular hand-picking may be sufficient; otherwise spray with malathion according to makers' instructions.

Celery leaf spot (*Septoria apiicola*) Fungus disease taking the form of small, brown patches with black specks. It spreads rapidly and can be fatal to the plants. Pick off and burn all affected leaves. Spraying with Bordeaux mixture or zineb in the early stages of growth is a good safeguard. If, however the seed has been bought from a reliable source it will have been treated against this disease and there should be no trouble. For this reason surplus celery seed should never be used in the kitchen.

Chafers Several species of beetle in the scarab family (SCARABAEIDAE), adults and larvae (grubs) of which attack leaves, flowers and roots of many garden plants. They are broad, thick-bodied beetles with strong, bristly legs, hard-furrowed wing-cases, and antennae with short comb-like tips. They are winged and fly by night, the large brown cockchafer being attracted to light and sometimes bumbling through an open window. They feed on leaves and flowers. The more familiar soil-living larvae are C-shaped, dirty white, fleshy with a brown head and legs. They feed on a wide variety of plant roots, rhizomes and tubers. Cockchafer (*Melolontha melolontha*) is the largest, 2·5–3·5cm (1–1$\frac{1}{3}$ in) long, pale reddish-brown, feeding on leaves of oak and other trees and shrubs; the large larvae eat roots of trees, shrubs (including fruit) and herbaceous plants. Garden chafer (*Phyllopertha horticola*) is about half the size of the cockchafer with a greenish head and thorax feeding also on flowers and young fruits; the larvae eat mainly grass roots, but also those of trees, shrubs, vegetables and ornamentals. Rose chafer (*Cetonia aurata*) is 1·5–

2cm ($\frac{3}{5}$–$\frac{4}{5}$ in) long, bright metallic-green all over and very conspicuous when feeding on a favourite rose blossom or other flowers such as raspberry and strawberry; the larvae feed on roots of trees, shrubs, etc, and perhaps also decaying vegetation – they are less of a pest than the previous species. These pests are difficult to eradicate as the adults are very mobile and the larvae often deep in the soil. For the latter apply HCH (BHC) dust according to maker's instructions and fork lightly into the soil surface. For the adults, spray with HCH liquid or malathion.

Chlorosis Yellowing of leaf and young shoot tissue due to lack of chlorophyll. Mineral deficiencies, viral and other diseases are largely responsible. Among the examples most commonly met with are lack of iron due to excess lime (mainly calcifuge plants), magnesium and manganese (fruit trees and other woody plants). See also Iron deficiency, Magnesium, manganese.

Chocolate spot One of the many manifestations of grey mould (*Botrytis cinerea*) showing on broadbean plants as chocolate streaking on the stems and blotching on the leaves. Most likely to be seen on overwintering plants after prolonged wet and cold, particularly on poor soils. Apply organic matter to the soil such as manure, garden compost, peat, etc, and give a dressing of a good general fertilizer.

Chrysanthemum Leaf Miner (*Phytomyza atricornis*) A common pest also attacking cinerarias and many other members of the daisy family (COMPOSITAE), including weeds such as groundsel and sow thistle. Damage shows as white or yellowish, sinuous lines caused by the tiny, legless larvae (grubs) tunnelling within the leaf tissue. Severe attacks weaken the plants and make them unsightly. When the grubs are mature they pupate and later emerge as small, dark-bodied true flies (order *Diptera*). Light attacks may be checked or stopped by picking and destroying infected leaves.

Above: adult leaf miners either lay their eggs on the surface of a leaf or insert them into the tissues; the larvae begin mining as soon as they hatch.

For heavier infestations spray with a liquid HCH (BHC) formulation or with malathion.

Clematis wilt The only serious disease that affects clematis. It usually occurs in the most mysterious way – the plant appears to be growing well and then suddenly all the foliage collapses, shrivels up and dies. In most cases, however, only part of the plant is affected. Treat by removing and burning all affected growth. If the diseased plant is growing on its own root system, it has a very good chance of recovering, since new growth normally appears from just below soil level. The disease appears to be caused by a fungus that is present in the soil. A preventative measure is to use a sulphur-based fungicide such as captan of dinocap. If clematis wilt has affected the plants in your garden in the past it is a good idea to spray the base of the clematis and the immediate surrounding soil at monthly intervals.

Club root (*Plasmodiophora brassicae*) Also known as finger and toe, this slime-mould fungus attacks the roots of many

Easily recognizable deficiencies in potassium (below), magnesium (below right), calcium (bottom) – can be prevented by using a good liquid feed.

Top: brassica with club root. These gall-like growths are caused by a fungus.
Top right: larva of codling moth in apple.
Above: the common cockroach.

Above: rash of coral spot fungus on a tree trunk. Although it lives mainly on dead wood, it can invade and kill adjacent living stems.

members of the family CRUCIFERAE, particularly brassicas and wallflower, causing gall-like growths on the main roots. Severely attacked plants are stunted and wilt badly in sunny weather. The fungus thrives in moist, acid soil and the best preventative is to apply garden lime at 500g per sq m (14 oz per sq yd) just before planting. If wet, the soil should be drained and lightened with organic matter, grit or weathered ashes. As a further precaution, dip the roots in mercurous chloride (calomel) or apply dazomet (Basamid) at planting time.

Cockroach Flattened, beetle-like insect in the family BLATTIDAE. It differs from beetles in having wing cases (elytra) that overlap down the middle of the back (those of beetles butting together neatly) and long, slender antennae. It is more nearly related to grasshoppers and crickets, and similarly has a biting mouth part. Several of the 3,500 species known have been introduced from warmer climates and are pests of warehouses and greenhouses. Although omnivorous and favouring dead animal remains, when short of food they will eat seedlings, young leaves and other tender living plant tissue. They are nocturnal and fast-moving, hiding by day. Commonest in Britain is the American cockroach (*Periplaneta americana*), with a body up to 3cm ($1\frac{1}{5}$ in) long, glossy brown with long bristly-spined legs. The common cockroach (*Blatta orientalis*) is 2cm ($\frac{4}{5}$ in) or more long and dull black, the female lacking wings and with rudimentary elytra. Keeping the greenhouse free of food and refuse that can act as hiding places will discourage these pests. Trapping is reasonably effective. Sink some jam jars into the floor baited with stale beer and treacle, or banana. HCH (BHC) and pyrethrum emulsion sprayed in all cracks and holes gives good control.

Codling moth (*Cydia pomonella*) A small member of the insect order *Lepidoptera*, the larvae of which feed in apple fruit and often cause premature drop. The moth with a wing span of about 1cm, ($\frac{2}{5}$ in), is brownish-grey with a rounded coppery patch towards the wing tips. Eggs are laid on or near young fruit and the larvae tunnel in and feed near the core. When fully grown they are pinkish-white with a brown head, 12–20mm ($\frac{1}{2}$-$\frac{4}{5}$in) long. They then leave the apple and spin a cocoon in bark crevices or debris on the ground. Pear, quince and walnut are also attacked sometimes. Spraying with malathion about four weeks after petal-fall and again three weeks later is recommended, but difficult to do properly on large trees. Where attacks are slight, trapping the larvae with bands of sacking tied around the trunk in late summer, and burning them in autumn, can be effective.

Copper Mineral salt of this metal is among the micronutrients or trace elements required for normal plant growth but in minute quantities. Most soils contain sufficient for most plants, but where there is a deficiency the primary symptom is a dieback of shoot tips. Summer dieback is a 'disease' of apples and pears. Shoots grow normally in spring but die back from the tips during summer. In some cases, particularly in various *Prunus* species, larger stems or branches may die accompanied by deformed shoots and gumming. Flower-bud formation is also inhibited.

Coral spot (*Nectria cinnabarina*) Allied to the cup fungi, this common fungus is easily identified by a rash of coral-red pustules or fruiting bodies, each 2–4mm ($\frac{1}{25}$ - $\frac{4}{25}$ in) wide, on dead twigs and branchlets of a wide selection of trees and shrubs. Although it lives mainly on dead wood, it can invade and kill adjacent living stems, so make sure that all dead growth is regularly removed and if cut surfaces are painted with white lead paint or a proprietary sealing compound damage will be prevented. Among the plants particularly susceptible are: red- and blackcurrants, gooseberry, plum, fig, walnut and apple.

Crane-fly Daddy longlegs: familiar, large, slender-bodied, long-legged fly

Top: leatherjacket, the grub or larva of the crane-fly. Centre: crane-fly of the genus Nephrotoma. *The yellow and black body gives it a superficial resemblance to a wasp and may help to protect it. Above: a cutworm.*

particularly abundant in late summer and autumn, the grub or larva of which is known as a leatherjacket. A member of the insect order *Diptera* (true flies), there are some 300 species in Britain and many more throughout the world. Only a few species are pests, notably common cranefly (*Tipula oleracea*), marsh cranefly (*T. paludosa*) and common spotted cranefly (*Nephrotoma maculata*), their leathery, grey or brownish, legless grubs 2·5–4cm (1–1$\frac{3}{5}$in) long when full-grown, feeding on plant roots, especially grasses.

Crown gall (*Agrobacterium tumefaciens*) (*Bacterium t.*) A parasitic organism, invisible to the naked eye, attacking the crowns or roots of a wide variety of herbaceous perennials and shrubs. The presence of the bacteria in the plant tissue probably causes the formation of a hormone that stimulates excessive cell division, resulting in the appearance of irregularly-rounded galls varying in size from a pea to a tennis ball or larger. The attacked plant may lack vigour but not invariably so. Infection occurs through wounds, especially on wet or very moist soils. Where crown gall is known to occur, roots of trees and shrubs, especially fruit, should be dipped in a proprietary fungicide before planting.

Crown rot General term for the rotting at ground level, or just below, of plants (such as rhubarb) with broad crowns. Several organisms can cause rotting, usually bacteria, which enter plant tissue via wounds especially in wet soils. All infected tissue should be cut away with a sharp knife and dusted with a fungicide such as captan. In the long term, drainage must be improved.

Cucumber mosaic virus A serious disease of cucumbers. Affected plants turn yellow, wilt and then die. Unfortunately, there is no cure. The virus is spread by aphids, and keeping the greenfly population down by spraying regularly with an insecticide such as derris or malathion is the best safeguard against the disease. Pull up and burn any infected plants as soon as they are seen.

Cutworm caterpillar of several species of noctuid moths that lurks in the surface layers of soil, feeding on roots and stems at soil level or on lower leaves after dark. The main species are heart and dart (*Agrotis exclamationis*), yellow underwing (*Noctua pronuba*) and turnip moth (*Euxoa segetum*). The caterpillars of heart, dart and turnip moths are a dirty grey, sometimes tinged brown, and about 3cm (1$\frac{1}{4}$ in) or more long; those of yellow underwing are larger, a dirty yellowish colour with a series of dark green or blackish stripes along the sides. They are most active from late summer to the following spring, when they pupate. The adult moths are on the wing from the first half of mid summer to the latter half of late summer, often with a partial second brood in early autumn. Favourite food plants include brassicas, turnip, lettuce, chrysanthemums, dahlias, China aster, *Zinnia*, polyanthus, beet. Control is not always easy; treat water-infected (wilting) plants with malathion or derris, or rake in HCH dust according to maker's instructions, but not on root vegetables such as carrots or potatoes, which this can taint.

Damping off Generally applied to seedlings or young plants when they rot off at ground level and collapse. Several fungi are responsible for this, notably *Pythium debaryanum* and, less commonly, *Rhizoctonia solani*. Both these fungi thrive in moist conditions, particularly where seedlings are overcrowded. Applying Cheshunt Compound or Quintozene (Botrilex) will stop further infection. To prevent attack, sow plants thinly, preferably in sterilized compost, and avoid over-watering.

Dieback Condition in which tree and shrub branches and shoots begin to die back from tips towards roots. Caused by bad soil conditions or, more commonly, by a fungus that enters through a wound. Cut out and burn infected wood and paint the cut with a protective paint. See entries on Anthracnose, Canker, Coral spot, Fireblight, Grey mould, Silver-leaf.

Drawn Used to describe plants grown under conditions of inadequate light,

Below: drawn onion seedlings which have been grown too close together.

showing as spindly, pale green shoots that frequently flop over. Many house plants show this condition when grown too far from a window. Seedlings may become drawn when grown too close together.

Drought Curiously enough, drought is seldom blamed for poor growth in British gardens. On free-draining soils in areas of least rainfall, eg East Anglia, drought is often an annual problem in late spring or summer. The situation is aggravated because so many of our best ornamental shrubs and perennials are native to areas of high rainfall and need plenty of water to thrive. When water is in really short supply, growth slows or stops and foliage lacks lustre and tends to wilt, particularly in sunshine. Under drier conditions still, leaves wilt permanently and may become dry and brown at the edges. Investigation of the soil will soon show if drought is the answer. Dig down to 10cm (4 in) and if the soil is dry all the way there is unlikely to be sufficient water lower down for normal growth. A really thorough soaking is the cure, ie not less than 23 litres per sq m ($4\frac{1}{2}$ gal per sq yd). Remember to check plants growing under high walls, overhanging eaves and trees, as they may well experience drought conditions when the rest of the garden is still all right.

Earthworm Well known creature belonging to the *Annelida,* a phylum of animals covering many sorts of segmented worms and leaches. There are many hundreds of different species, some 220 in Europe alone, with about 25 of these in Britain, and they are found in all but the most acid soils. They are useful members of the fauna of undisturbed soils, particularly meadowland where their tunnels provide drainage and aeration channels, and their habit of dragging dead leaves and other plant fragments into their tunnels adds to the humus-content of the soil. Worms move through the soil partly by forcing a way, but largely by eating themselves forward. In doing this they take in a mixture of fine organic and mineral particles that on passing through the body often have a better structure than the surrounding soil and are richer in plant food. For this reason, worm-casts swept from the lawn should not be discarded but used as a top-

Top: an earthworm is beneficial to the garden although its casts may be unsightly. Centre: the common earwig (Forficula auricularia). *Above: a mass of nematodes of the species* Trichodorus viruliferus, *each less than 1mm long, attacking the root of an apple tree. The ginger-coloured area is dead plant cells.*

dressing or placed on the compost heap. Only two of the British species regularly make casts, the remainder excreting below soil-level. In the regularly cultivated flower or vegetable plot where organic matter is dug in, worms have less to contribute. If a lawn of fine grasses and immaculate appearance is desired, worm-casts can be a nuisance, and if it is considered necessary, one of the modern worm-killers such as carbaryl can be used to maker's instructions. Alternatively, the old fashioned and less poisonous mowrah meal can be applied and watered in, and then the quickly exiting worms swept up and removed.

Earwig Member of the insect order *Dermaptera,* largely typified by an elongated, glossy brown body, short wing-case like a small waistcoat, and pincers at the tail (abdomen) end. About 1000 different kinds are known but only four of these occur in Britain and two are rare. The common earwig (*Forficula auricularia*) is about 1·5cm ($\frac{3}{5}$ in) long excluding antennae, the female with slim, straight pincers, the male with more robust, curved ones. It hides in cracks and crannies by day, feeding at night on carrion, other insects and plants, particularly petals of flowers. In some years it is more abundant and can be a severe pest on a wide variety of flowers, particularly chrysanthemum and dahlia. Traps provide a moderately effective control, provided they are emptied daily into boiling water. Stuff small tins or flower pots with wood-wool or straw and invert on the plant stake or canes specially provided. Alternatively apply HCH (BHC) dust.

Eelworm Microscopic, colourless, worm-like creatures belonging to the phylum *Nematoda* and thus in no way to be confused with earthworms. Also known as nematodes, they parasitize a wide variety of plants, some species attacking within stems and leaves, others roots, rhizomes, bulbs, causing stunting, wilting and eventual death. There is no effective chemical control but infected plants that are not too weakened and are valuable, may be given hot water treatment (immersing at 46°C (115°F) for 5 minutes in the case of chrysanthemum eelworm, for example) with a good chance of success. The most important eelworms are: **1** Chrysanthemum (*Aphelenchoides ritzemabosi*), which attacks also calceolarias, china asters, peonies etc, first causing brown to black areas between leaf veins. **2** Leaf blotch (*A. fragariae, syn. A. olesistus*), which attacks greenhouse ferns, begonias, gloxinias, coleus, also strawberries and other soft fruit outside causing black and brown leaf blotches or (particularly on ferns) striping and crippling of young leaves and shoots. **3** Potato cyst (*Heterodera rostochiensis)*, which also attacks tomatoes, invading the root system where it forms tiny yellow or brown, seed-like cysts; plants are yellow, stunted, and often collapse and die. The cysts contain eggs and can be dormant in the soil for years after the plant has died, so it is important not to grow the same crop on infected land. **4** Root knot (*Meloidogyne* species), particularly a pest of cucumbers and tomatoes under glass, attacking the roots and forming lumpy galls; leaves become discoloured and vigour is diminished, but the plants often grow moderately well. **5** Stem and bulb (*Ditylenchus dipsaci*), probably the worst eelworm in Britain with several biological races infecting a wide range of plants, including narcissus, phlox, strawberries, onions and many weeds; infestation causes the plant tissue to become distorted, then soft and rotten, the plant finally collapsing; infected plants must be removed and the area kept free of weed hosts.

Fasciation Freakish, flattened or crested conditions of plants, often seeming as though several stems or shoots have been squashed together. This appears to result from an irritation of the minute growing points of stems and buds by fungi, mites or bacteria, but there is little scientific evidence. Another known cause is genetic mutation, probably resulting from natural cosmic radiation. In this category is the cock's comb plant (*Celosia argentea cristata*), that now comes true from seed. Fasciation has resulted in several cultivars of succulents and shrubs grown for curiosity, eg *Notocactus leninghausii* Cristata, *Salix sachalinensis* Sekka, and *Sedum reflexum* Cristatum. The condition often occurs on the hybrid spring bell (*Forsythia* × *intermedia* Spectabilis).

Fireblight (*Erwinia amylovora*) Bacterial disease, primarily attacking woody members of the rose family, notably pear and some species of *Cotoneaster, Crataegus, Malus, Pyracantha, Sorbus* etc. Disease symptoms start as a withering and blackening of flowers, followed by death of the spurs and lateral twigs. The bark of infected branches turns grey-black and cankers appear, the dead tissues of which, plus hanging bunches of brown, withered leaves, give a scorched appearance. You can check if the disease is present by peeling back the bark – the wood appears reddish brown if it is infected. There is no effective cure; dig up and burn infected trees. In Britain statutory regulations under the Fireblight Disease Order require that any outbreak of this disease should be immediately reported to the authorities.

Flea beetle Several species of small jumping beetle in the *Chrysomelidae*, a family of leaf-eaters. Best-known are several species of *Phyllotreta*, metallic-black or blue-black, sometimes with two broad, yellow stripes down the back (wing cases), and rarely more than 3mm ($\frac{1}{8}$in) long. They attack seedling brassicas, eating out numerous small holes, and can do severe damage in dry spells from late spring to autumn. They are easily controlled by dusting with HCH (BHC) dust or spraying with derris.

Above: moderately severe flea beetle damage on radish seedlings.

Frit fly Also known as oat fly and primarily a farm pest of oats and other cereals, this tiny fly also attacks sweetcorn. The first visible symptoms of attack are creamy-yellow streaks on young leaves. Later, the leaves break up into frayed strips. Plants remain more or less stunted and cobs are fewer. In very severe cases the growing point is killed and the whole plant may die. The black bodied fly (*Oscinella frit*) is only 1·5mm ($\frac{1}{16}$in) long and resembles a small midge. It lays eggs at the bases of young plants from April to June. In areas where it is known to occur, frit fly can be prevented by dusting the plants with HCH as soon as they are planted out, repeating after rain until early June.

Gall Swelling that may occur on any part of a plant but mostly on stems and leaves. Galls form as the result of irritation set up by bacteria, fungi, eelworms, mites and various insects, and are of various shapes and colours. The presence of galls on garden plants is harmful in comparatively few cases although sometimes unsightly. See entry for Midge, Big-bud and Crown gall.

Above: lime leaves with nail gall swellings. Although sometimes unsightly, the presence of galls on garden plants is rarely harmful.

Gladiolus diseases 1 Dry rot (*Sclerotinia gladioli*). First observed as premature leaf yellowing, this fungus primarily attacks the corm, causing black spots and blotches. Severe infection kills the corm, turning it into a blackened mummified object. All plants that yellow prematurely in summer should be dug up and destroyed. Corms from plants nearby should be examined when lifting, the fibrous skin or tunic removed first; if black spots or streaks are seen, destroy –or, if valuable cultivars, treat with benomyl (Benlate). **2** Neck rot and scab (*Bacterium marginatum*) is first noticed as soft rot at ground level, often causing toppling of the whole plant. Corms show small, crater-like depressions with prominent rims. Removal of these with the tip of a sharp knife and dusting with powdered sulphur will save the corms if they are not too severely infected. **3** Leaf spot or hard rot (*Septoria gladioli*) shows as a brown flecking on the foliage. Later the corms develop firm black sunken areas and death eventually results. Remove these black areas and treat with benomyl.

Gooseberry dieback: (*Botrytis cinerea*) This sometimes serious disease of gooseberry bushes is an expression of the grey mould fungus. Gaining entry into the plant by pruning cuts or breaks, it causes first a browning, next a whitening of leaf margins followed by withering, and then death of the stems or branches beyond the point of infection. If infection is near ground level the whole bush will die. Pruning away all growth below the point of infection is the only remedy. Make sure that all pruning cuts are protected by using a proprietary wound paint, white-lead paint or a grafting wax or compound.

Gooseberry mildew: American gooseberry mildew (*Sphaerotheca mors-uvae*) is one of the worst diseases of the gooseberry, causing a white, powdery coating followed by distortion and crippling of stems and sometimes dieback; fruit is spoiled and bushes weakened. Spray at first sight of the disease with dinocap or lime-sulphur, or washing soda on sulphur-shy cultivars; 30g washing soda to 1 litre water (1 oz to 1¾ pints), plus a wetting agent, applied just before blossoming and again when the fruit has set.

Gooseberry sawfly, *see* Sawflies.

Grape splitting A condition arising when the grapes are 'overcharged' with sap. In this event, leave about one-third of the flowering laterals unstopped in the following year, to absorb sap that would otherwise have gone to the grapes.

Greenback Not a disease but a condition. Affected fruits have a hard, yellow patch which refuses to ripen. It may be caused by too much sun, or lack of potash. Eurocross and Alicante are among several modern varieties which are resistant to greenback.

Grey bulb rot This disease (*Rhizoctonia tuliparum*) mainly attacks tulip bulbs, but bulbous iris, ixia, colchicum, crocus, hyacinthus, narcissus and lilies can also be hosts. Infected bulbs fail to grow and when dug up have a dry rot with soil particles adhering. Usually there is a whitish mould among which are rounded to flattened resting bodies each up to 8cm (3 in) long, white at first, then black. Attacked bulbs and adjacent soil must be removed and destroyed (burnt). There is no chemical control suitable for the home gardener. Susceptible bulbs should not be planted in the same place for at least five years.

Above: honey fungus can effect severe damage to trees and shrubs.

Grey mould, *see* Botrytis.

Honey fungus (*Armillaria mellea*) Also known as bootlace fungus, this parasitic ally of the mushroom mainly attacks trees and shrubs but sometimes infects herbaceous plants such as rhubarb and bulbs. It can live in dead tree stumps and roots, sending out tough, black, bootlace-like structures called rhizomorphs that then attack living roots; it spreads upwards under the bark as a lacy network of white threads. Attacked plants or branches usually wilt quite suddenly and soon die. Yellow-brown or honey-coloured, edible, toadstool fruiting bodies, 4–10cm (1½–4 in) wide, are produced in dense clusters, usually from the bases of dead plants or buried roots, in summer and autumn. This fungus is often worse in badly drained areas and is more likely to attack weak plants or through damaged roots. It is not easily eradicated, but Armillatox and Bray's Emulsion have proved effective under ideal conditions.

Ink disease (*Drechslera iridis*) Likely to be encountered more in the north and west where conditions are cooler and wetter. Winter flowering and Dutch irises are worst affected. Young leaves may bear yellow streaks which soon develop into black blotches after they expand above the soil. The bulbs too bear black patches and streaks followed by death of the tissues. Severely attacked bulbs must be destroyed, those showing early foliage symptoms may be saved by spraying with dichlofluanid at two-weekly intervals.

Iron The mineral salt of this metal is one of the micronutrients or trace elements essential for the functioning of all green

Above: pale sinuous lines left by the larva of a leaf miner on a brassica leaf. Left: blotches mined by the fly Phytomyza ilicis *on a holly leaf.*

plants as it enters into the formation of chlorophyll. Iron deficiency shows as yellow to white shoot tips that may later turn brown and die back. In already developed leaves, the veins remain green, with all the tissue in between yellow. Trees and shrubs are most likely to suffer deficiency especially on chalky or other dry, limey soils. The remedy is to apply a chelated iron compound (Sequestrene) or sulphate of iron at 120g per sq m (4 oz per sq yd).

Leaf blotches and spots Various fungi and viruses cause yellow, brown and black spots or larger blotches to form on leaves. Very obvious examples are black spot of roses (qv) and the tar spot of maples. The latter (*Rhytisma acerinum*), is mainly on sycamore (*Acer pseudoplatanus*) where it forms large tar-black blotches. It is difficult to cure, but Bordeaux mixture used at three-weekly intervals during the summer is sometimes effective. Other spot and blotch diseases, eg on celery, cherry, chrysanthemum, iris, pelargonium (geranium), tomato and arum lily usually respond to treatment with zineb, thiram, captan, benomyl or Bordeaux mixture.

Leaf miner Tiny grub or caterpillar, of certain species of moth, beetle, true fly and sawfly, that feeds within the leaf tissue. As a result of its feeding activities either pale sinuous lines or blotches appear. Severe attacks, particularly of blotch miners such as celery fly (qv) can weaken plants and render them unsightly. Among the more obvious blotch miners are holly l.m. caused by the fly *Phytomyza ilicis;* lilac l.m. by the moth *Gracilaria syringella,* which also attacks privet and rolls the leaf tips when too large to mine; and birch l.m. by the sawfly *Phyllotoma nemorata.* Sinuous or linear miners include chrysanthemum, by the fly *Phytomyza atricornis;* columbine l.m. by *P. aquilegiae,* and pea l.m. by *P. pisi,* cabbage l.m. (also on other members of the same family – CRUCIFERAE), by the large striped flea beetle; and rose l.m. by the moth *Nepticula anomalella.* Because they feed between the waxy upper and lower leaf epidermises, leaf mining creatures are difficult to eradicate. Regular hand picking can be effective, and several chemical substances are reasonably efficient, eg malathion, nicotine and the systemic dimethoate (Rogor E).

Leaf mould (*Fulvia fulva*) A serious disease of greenhouse tomatoes. The symptoms are a greyish mould on the underside of the leaves with yellow patches on the upper surface. Remove and burn affected leaves and spray with a systemic fungicide. A stagnant atmosphere, especially at night, is the cause and adequate ventilation is the best safeguard. The disease is more prevalent in some areas than in others; if you know it to be troublesome in your district, spray with the fungicide in mid-summer and again in late summer as a precautionary measure. The variety Supercross (F.1 hybrid) and some strains of Eurocross are immune.

Leatherjacket *see* Crane fly.

Lily Beetle *(Crioceris lilii)* True beetle *(Coleoptera)* belonging to the leaf-eating family CHRYSOMELIDAE, grubs (larvae) of which live on species of *Lilium, Fritillaria, Nomocharis* and *Polygonatum.* The adult beetle is oblong, scarlet except for a small black head. The grubs are short and hump-backed, dirty white to yellow, feeding conspicuously. This pest is very localized in Britain, occurring mainly in the south-east, but can appear almost anywhere that lilies and their allies are grown. It is easily controlled by spraying with malathion, or by hand-picking if the infestation is small.

Lily Disease *(Botrytis elliptica)* A serious disease of many lilies, particularly *L. candidum* and *L. regale*, starting as water-soaked spots on leaves, the spots later becoming greyish or whitish. After this, the leaves become brownish and rot, the grey, fluffy sporing mould appearing; if stems are attacked they later topple over and plants are greatly weakened. It is worst of all in wet seasons or where air circulation is poor. At the first sign, spray with Bordeaux mixture or a liquid copper formulation.

Lime *see* Calcium.

Magnesium One of the major mineral elements required for plant growth. It is essential for certain enzymes involved in the movement of phosphates in the plant and is a part of chlorophyll. Deficiency shows first in the older leaves as severe chlorosis or a chlorotic pattern between the veins with the margins staying green. Chlorotic areas often turn brown (necrosis) and leaves fall prematurely.

Below: apple leaves suffering from a deficiency in magnesium.

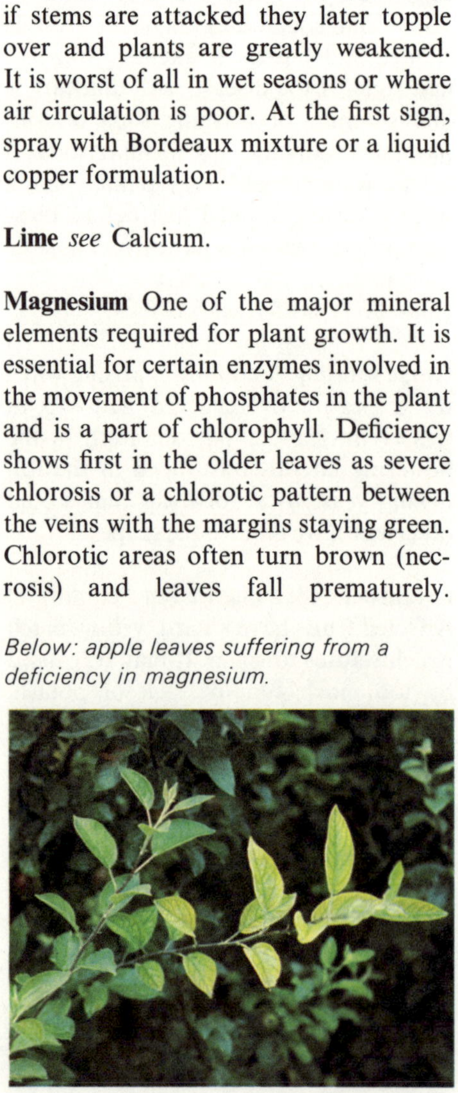

Left: a rabbit guard protects a young sapling. Above: tree damage caused by fallow deer. The bark is completely stripped, killing the young pine tree.

Remedy by applying Epsom salts (magnesium sulphate) at 30g per sq m (1 oz per sq yd), repeating annually, or spray foliage with solution of 30g Epsom salts dissolved in 1 litre of water (1 oz in 1½ pints) plus a spreader.

Mammals Rabbit, hare, grey squirrel, wood mouse, short-tailed vole, mole, deer, dog and cat are or can be pests in the garden. The damage they do is obvious. The cures are various and not always easy to provide. Where rabbits are abundant the only cure is to fence with 2·5–3cm (1–1⅕ in) mesh chicken wire. This must be at least 1·2m (4 ft) wide, 30cm (1 ft) of it buried in the ground, the rest supported by stakes. Where rabbits are fewer, choice plants can be guarded with collars of chicken wire and tree stems given spiral protectors. Hares can be kept out in the same way, but where they are locally abundant boundary fences will need to be at least 1·2m (4ft) above the ground but only a few centimetres (1–2 in) buried. Mice and voles can be reduced by trapping but make sure the traps are placed where birds and domestic pets cannot get at them. The same goes for the poisonous warfarin baits. Wire mesh with 1cm (½ in) holes will protect bulbs and corms, either laid over each clump or drift and covered with a little soil or fashioned into boxes or 'hats' buried in the ground. Voles like dense ground vegetation, ideally rough grassland. Keeping grass of this kind short, or removing it, often reduces the voles. Moles are the most difficult to eliminate, especially in favourable areas where there is a naturally high population in adjacent grass or woodland. Traps are not easy to set and are often avoided by a wary mole. Poisoning by strychnine needs a licence and should be done by an expert. Smoke cartridges and other deterrents may not work or may succeed for a short time only. Beds of special small plants can be protected by ringing with strips of chicken wire buried at least 30cm (1ft) deep and ideally, twice this. Young trees and shrubs can be established in a mole-ridden area by lining the planting holes with chicken wire. Where they are a trouble on lawns and if trapping fails, applying a worm-killer regularly to eliminate the mole's food often reduces or stops their tunnelling activities. Deer can be a serious nuisance if there is a resident herd nearby. In such a case high wire mesh fencing is the only deterrent. Specimen trees can be safeguarded by using the spiral trunk protectors. Other people's dogs and cats can be the worst sort of pest that any keen gardener can have, especially in suburbia. Close mesh fencing at least 90cm (3 ft) and preferably 1·2m (4 ft) tall will keep most dogs at bay. Fencing is no good against cats and reliance must be placed on pepper dust and other repellents, which don't always seem to work very well. Newly raked and sown areas should be kept watered as this tends to discourage the scratching habit that cats are best known for, or you could try inserting sticks until the seedlings are established.

Manganese One of the trace or micronutrient elements needed for plant growth, being essential for certain enzymes and chloroplasts. Deficiency symptoms vary. In trees and shrubs chlorosis is common particularly on older leaves, starting at leaf margins and progressing in v-patterns inwards between the veins. On potatoes, spots and lesions (speckled yellows) appear beside the leaf veins, while in peas and beans dead brown areas form on the cotyledons within the seed, a disorder known as marsh spot. The remedy is to wet the soil with manganese sulphate at 30g dissolved in 2 litres (1 oz per 1¾ pints) of water. On very limy soils (pH 7 or above), it is recommended to apply manganese in a chelated, sequestered or fritted form.

Above: blackberry suffering from a manganese deficiency.

Mealy bugs A familiar sight on a wide variety of plants under glass, mealy bugs are tropical and subtropical in origin and are seldom seen outside. At least four different species of *Pseudococcus* can be found but an expert is needed to name them accurately. They are members of the same order as capsid bugs and aphids (*Hemiptera*) but are more sedentary creatures. Soft bodied and oval in shape they cluster together in leaf axils and crevices in stems protected by waxy filaments and powder. Their sap sucking weakens the plant and the honeydew they secrete encourages sooty mould (qv). Malathion, dimethoate, formothion all give a fairly good cure. Severe attacks on stems should be removed with a soft brush dipped in spray strength insecticide or methylated spirit. *Rhizoecus* mealy bugs live on roots of pot plants. They can be killed by watering with spray strength insecticide.

Midge General name for many true flies (insect order *Diptera*) belonging to several families and including the unpleasantly familiar biting midge. Horticulturally (and agriculturally), one family – the CECIDOMYIIDAE (gall midges) – provides several plant pests. The adults are small to minute, only a few millimetres (under $\frac{1}{5}$ in) long, and seldom observed. The females insert eggs into plant tissue by means of an ovipositor, and the developing larvae (maggots) irritate the plant, causing characteristic galls to form. In general the larvae are short, cylindrical, legless, and often a shade of red. Although several midge species are agricultural pests, only a few are a nuisance to the gardener: **pear midge** (*Contarinia pyricora*), where the eggs are laid in the flowers and the white larvae tunnel into the developing fruitlets, which become swollen and distorted, later cracking, decaying and falling – spray with malathion or HCH (BHC) immediately after petal-fall, and rake up and burn all fallen fruitlets; **pear leaf curling midge** (*Dasyneura pyri* and sometimes other species), where the eggs are laid as the leaves unfold and the whitish larvae cause marginal curl which, in severe cases, results in the whole leaf-blade becoming tightly rolled, later blackening and dying – if this pest is known to be present, spray at 2–3 weekly intervals with malathion or HCH, starting as the leaves unfurl; **violet midge** (*Dasyneura affinis*), where the eggs are laid within unfurling leaves and the orange larvae cause marginal curl and a thickening and distortion of the tissue – in severe attacks, leaves are totally rolled and even the flowers are distorted, so pick off all infected leaves and dig out severely attacked plants and burn, then spraying with malathion according to maker's instructions at 2–3 weekly intervals.

Below: pupae of the midge Forcipomyia, *which bites humans but is harmless to plants. Below right: powdery mildew on a rose. Above right: sphagnum moss.*

Mildew Popular vernacular name used loosely for any small fungus, the hyphae of which form greenish, whitish or brownish patches on damp wallpaper, leather, food and plants. Most of these are really moulds and of little concern to gardeners. True mildews are parasitic fungi mainly affecting leaves, young shoots and fruit. They show as a whitish or grey-white powdery covering or patches, the tissue beneath turning yellow or purplish and often becoming distorted. Premature leaf-fall may result. There are two main groups: **1** powdery, living on the leaf or shoot surface, sending down minute feeding suckers (haustoria) into the epidermis cells; **2** downy, living deep within the leaf or shoot cells, often less conspicuous and sometimes showing first as yellow patches, the greyish or glaucous mealy hyphae and spores appearing on the underside of the leaves. Where mildew is prevalent in greenhouses avoid sudden drops of temperature and ventilate more freely and regularly. Powdery mildews can usually be controlled by spraying with dinocap (Karathane or Crotothane) or benomyl (Benlate). Downy mildews do not always respond so well to spraying, although thiram (Ferna-col, Fernasan) and zineb (Dyblite) are usually effective. Severely infected leaves and shoots are best removed before spraying.

Mint rust, *see* Rust Fungus.

Molybdenum Micronutrient or trace element concerned with the functioning of at least three oxidizing enzymes within the plant. Symptoms of deficiency vary from plant to plant and are not fully known for most ornamentals. In some cases leaves fail to develop properly, eg Whiptail 'disease' of cauliflower where the leaf-blade is largely missing, leaving a whip-like mid-rib. Growing points may die and a chlorotic mottling occurs on tomato and lettuce leaves. Tomato leaves may also roll inwards. In addition, nodule-dwelling nitrogen-fixing bacteria fail to function properly and leguminous plants can show nitrogen deficiency. Remedy by applying sodium molybdate: 30g dissolved in 1 litre of water will treat 10 sq m of soil (1 oz per $1\frac{3}{4}$ pt per 11 sq yd).

Mosaic Name given to a widespread group of viruses, the best known being cucumber mosaic. This starts as a yellow flecking on the leaves which spreads into large blotches which may fuse. Individual leaves are greatly reduced in size and the whole plant is stunted. The fruits may be pitted or deformed. This virus attacks a wide range of plants including anemones, aquilegias, begonias, dahlias, lettuce, lilies, marrows, narcissi, nicotianas, petunias, spinach, tomatoes, tulips, violas and zandedeschias. It also occurs in various weeds and wild plants, eg white bryony, teasel. Aphids are the primary spreaders of cucumber mosaic and keeping greenfly down will reduce the chance of attack. Infected plants must be destroyed. Arabis mosaic is similar in its symptoms. It has little effect on arabis itself, but causes yellow dwarf disease of raspberry, and also attacks strawberry. Infected plants must be destroyed.

Moss Primitive, spore-bearing plant that, together with the liverworts, makes up the order *Bryophyta*. It forms mats or cushions of erect to prostrate thread-like stems bearing translucent, awl or scale-like, generally overlapping leaves of one cell thickness. The visible moss plant is the sexual or gametophyte generation and equivalent to the prothallus of a fern. Minute 'flowers', usually at the tips of

the shoots, give rise to the spore-bearing generation (sporophyte) that comprises the familiar spore capsule and its stalk of attachment. For comments on the nuisance value of mosses on seed pots and container-grown plants, see Liverwort in Weeds section.

Mushroom flies *see* Sciarid Flies.

Narcissus basal rot (*Fusarium oxysporum*) Disease that can be serious on daffodils and narcissi and, less frequently, on crocus and lachanalia. Narcissus and daffodil bulbs show the main symptoms after lifting and during summer storage. The basal plate or ring of the bulb softens and turns deep brown. Later, the rot spreads through the bulb and often takes on a red-purple hue. Crocus are infected earlier, the foliage yellowing and dying prematurely. Lifted corms have a basal rot which spreads upwards as brown strands in the corm tissue. Later, a covering of pink-tinted mycelium may develop. Infected bulbs and corms must be destroyed and, ideally, the site used to grow something else for about three years. Alternatively, fresh bulbs can be steeped in a suspension of benomyl or thiophanate-methyl for at least 15 minutes before planting.

Narcissus fly Bulbs that fail to grow or produce only a few narrow, yellowish, crippled leaves are likely to be suffering from narcissus fly. The bulbs feel soft and when cut open reveal greyish-brown fly grubs surrounded by wet, rotted bulb tissue. Three species are involved, the large narcissus fly (*Merodon equestris*), which is rather like a small bumble bee, and the two small narcissus flies (*Eumerus strigatus*) and *E. tuberculatus* which are only half the size. The large narcissus fly lays eggs singly at the base of a daffodil plant or in the hole left by the withered leaves. The small flies lay eggs in batches of six or more. Control is not easy. Where this pest is known to occur, the soil should be dusted with HCH and the holes left by withered leaves raked over to discourage egg laying. Any soft bulbs should be discarded.

Narcissus viruses Several virus diseases afflict daffodils and narcissi, two of them being common and widespread. Yellow stripe virus causes yellowish streaks and curling of the leaves plus crippling of the flowers. White streak starts as purple streaks in the leaves which later turn white, expand and fuse together. As a result the leaves die off before their usual time and the bulbs are weakened. Both viruses are spread by aphids. Infected bulbs must be destroyed and new replacements kept sprayed against aphids.

Necrosis Necrotic: dead or dying tissue, generally as the result of disease or extreme mineral deficiency. It may be an overall effect as in a severe case of potato blight, or mottling or flecking. In either case it usually starts as a yellowing or discoloration that browns and then blackens. Although usually an external symptom, localized necrosis can also affect inner tissues, as in bitterpit of apples or internal rust spots in potatoes.

Nitrogen Among the most important of all the major nutrient elements, and essential for the formation of proteins that in turn are constituents of protoplasm, the life stuff of all plants. Deficiency results in suppression of growth, stems being short, thin and stiff, leaves small, pale or yellowish-green, later developing tints of red, yellow, orange or purple. Flower-bud formation is reduced and their opening delayed; fruiting and tuber formation are poor. Deficiency is rectified with a dressing of one of the nitrogen fertilizers, eg sulphate of ammonia.

Nut drop Brown rot fungus (qv) enters cob and hazel nuts by the hole bored by the nut weevil, and the nut then rots. Control the weevil. Be careful not to damage the tree as fungus can enter through any wounds.

Nut weevil (*Curculio nucum*) This bores a hole in the soft shell in spring and lays an egg. The resultant grub feeds on the nut. To control this, spray with derris in early to mid summer (late May to early June), and again about two weeks later. Spraying may not be needed every year. To determine whether weevils are present or absent lay a sheet under the bush in early summer (late May) and strike the bush sharply. If weevils are there, they will fall on to the sheet. In this event expect an attack, and spray accordingly.

Onion fly (*Delia antiqua*) Member of the insect order *Diptera* (true flies) and the most serious of all onion pests. The legless, white larvae (maggots) tunnel into the young, or just forming, onion bulbs, reducing them to a soft, decaying mass. The leaves rapidly turn yellow or whitish and collapse. The adult is not unlike a small, greyish-bodied house-fly. There are usually three broods a year, the last one overwintering in the pupal state. If this pest is known to be troublesome, grow plants from sets or autumn-sown seed that is generally less often attacked. When thinning, avoid bruising the plants more than necessary as the smell attracts adult insects. The insecticide trichlorphon (Dipterex) gives good control but at present is not available in small packs.

Parsnip canker Disease of parsnips, of fungal origin with three distinct types

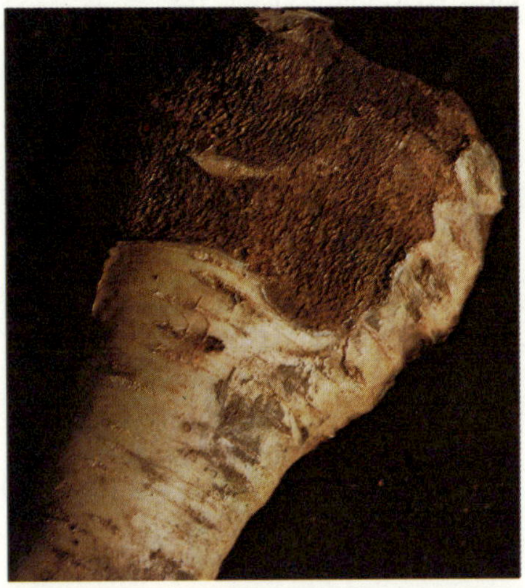

of fungus mainly involved. *Itersonilia pastinacea* causes black canker. This starts as leaf spotting and spores from the spots wash down into the soil, infecting roots where wounds have been made by soil insects. Small blackish lesions result. *Mycocentrospora acerina* causes purplish lesions and is the commonest canker in very humus-rich soil. *Phoma* is less common but also causes black lesions. Where canker is a problem it is best to grow the resistant cultivar 'Avon Resister'. Cultural conditions are important. Parsnips should only be grown in well-drained soils. Carrot fly grubs make wounds suitable for the canker fungi, so this pest must be controlled. Small roots from late sown seed seem to suffer very little from canker and it is advisable to delay sowing until the end of April or May.

Pea moth (*Cydia nigricana*) makes its appearance when flowering begins and the grubs may be found inside the pods. Spray the flowers with a reliable insecticide as they open, and again 10 days later. Peas that mature in autumn (August or September) are seldom attacked.

Pea, and Bean Weevil *see* Weevil.

Peach leaf curl (*Taphgrina deformans*). Unsightly and weakening disease of peaches, nectarines, apricots and almonds, showing as grossly distorted, red-flushed leaves. Control by spraying with lime sulphur, liquid copper or Bordeaux mixture just before leaf-fall and again in late winter or early spring, ideally two applications each time with about 10–14 days between.

Above: the distorted, red flushed leaves produced by peach leaf curl. Left: root afflicted with parsnip canker.

Peony blight or wilt (*Botrytis paeoniae*). Disease that attacks herbaceous peonies at or near ground level, and tree peonies on or just below the flower-buds, causing collapse and death of tissue beyond the point of infection. Damage can be severe in wet years, especially on heavy soils. Dead tissue becomes covered with typical grey mould sporing bodies. Cut off all infected stems below the point of infection as soon as possible and apply copper dust. If the disease is of regular occurrence spray with thiram or zineb as soon as the young leaves expand in spring and repeat at two-weekly intervals until flower-buds show colour.

Petal blight Several fungus diseases attack flowers, either killing whole buds or blooms or seriously spoiling some or all petals. Grey mould (*Botrytis cinerea*) is the main offender but a few others are troublesome. Chrysanthemum petal blight (*Itersonilia perplexans*) causes small rusty spots or larger semi-transparent blotches or lesions. Later, the petals shrivel and brown; eventually the whole bloom dies. Grey mould may come in at this point masking the real trouble. Zineb is an efficient cure if applied the moment the first symptoms are seen and continued at two-weekly interludes. Chrysanthemum ray blight (*Didymella chrysanthemi*) starts like petal blight but affects leaves too. Immature buds may rot and the leaf spotting develops into areas of blackish decay. Diseased plants should be destroyed, the remainder sprayed with thiram or zineb.

Phosphorus Member of the major nutrient elements essential for plant growth. It enters into the complex process of photosynthesis and is a constituent of protoplasm, the life stuff of plants. Deficiency results in small, thin shoots and leaves, the latter either with a bluish cast, tinted purple or bronze, or developing marginal scorch (potato) or brown spotting (blackcurrant). Flower-bud formation is poor, resulting in low fruit and seed yields; tuber production is also poor. Deficiency is rectified with a dressing of superphosphate, basic slag or steamed bone flour.

Plum Sawfly, *see* Sawflies.

Potash Mineral form of the metal element potassium in combination with oxygen and other substances, eg sulphate, chloride, phosphate, nitrate and carbonate. It is naturally present in all soils in varying amounts, those derived from clay being richest. Quite often, though, the amount of potassium available to plant roots is inadequate for fully healthy growth. Among the more concentrated supplies of potash are the mineral deposits mined in Germany and elsewhere, extracted and sold as sulphate of potash. Burnt remains, particularly of seaweeds, salt marsh and other green plants (but very little in pure wood ash, contrary to popular thought) can yield up to 5 per cent potash in the highly soluble carbonate combination. Ashes

Below: a chrysanthemum flower suffering from petal blight.

of this sort can be liberally applied to soil deficient in potash, but the purer sulphate of potash should not exceed 30g per sq m (1 oz per sq yd) annually. There must also be a certain amount of lime in the soil for the potassium to become readily available and be absorbed by the plant roots.

Potassium Member of the major nutrient elements essential for plant growth. It is a necessary constituent of the nuclei of cells and is needed for the functioning of several essential enzymes resulting in the formation of starches, sugars and fibrous tissue. Deficiency results in lack of vigour and thin shoots with short internodes: leaves may have a bluish or yellowish cast followed by brown margins or tips (leaf scorch and tip burn); brown spotting (necrosis) may also occur. Shoot tips may die and fruiting is poor in more advanced examples. A dressing of potash fertilizer will cure deficiency.

Potato blight, *see* Blight.

Potato blackleg (*Erwinia carotovora atroseptica*) Bacterial disease that often permeates the whole plant causing stunting and yellow-green foliage, the plant finally collapsing and dying, with the base of the stem turning soft and black. Tubers may also be infested and if so, often rot in store. Destroy all infected plants as soon as recognized and start again with fresh tubers. The bacteria can only survive on tubers or plants so there is no risk of the soil becoming contaminated. However, because of tubers that might be left in the ground after lifting, it is advisable to grow potatoes in a different site for at least one season.

Potato viruses Potatoes can be attacked by about ten different viruses, five of which are common or fairly so. Leaf roll virus causes upward rolling of the leaflets which become stiff and rattle when the plant is shaken. Virus Y starts as dark streaks or spots in the leaflets which then yellow and shrivel. The second year plants are stunted, with yellow-green puckered leaves and a few small tubers only. Virus X and/or A, are less easy to diagnose, producing as visual symptoms a pale mottle often only visible on a dull day. The tuber yield may be greatly reduced. Tobacco rattle can be recognised by the small yellowish rings on the leaves and corky crescent-shaped brownish marks in the flesh of the tuber. These symptoms indicate one form of a disease known as spraing. Mop top is also known as spraing but differs from tobacco rattle in the addition of blistery rings on the tubers (not always present) and yellow V-shaped marks on the leaves. When fully developed the haulm takes on a mop-like appearance. Plants infected by any of these viruses must be destroyed and on no account must small tubers be saved for "seed" to plant again. Viruses A, X and Y are spread by aphids, so eliminating these insects will help.

Below: a potato plant suffering from leaf roll virus.

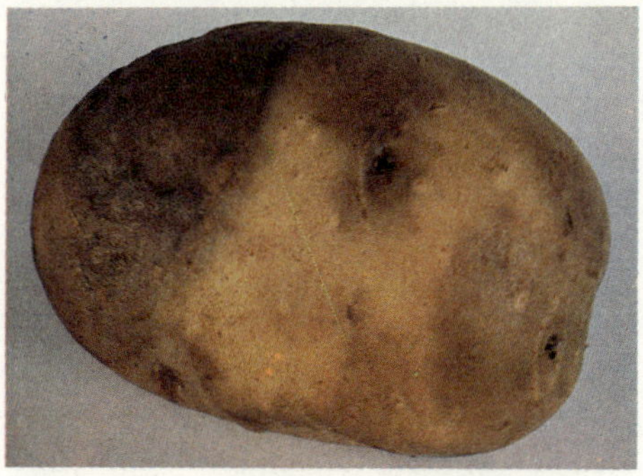

Above: young tuber affected by a fungus related potato blight.

Raspberry Beetle (*Byturus tomentosus*) A bad attack of raspberry beetle can be disastrous and render the entire crop useless. The beetles hibernate in the soil over winter and emerge in early summer (May). They lay their eggs in the very heart of the flowers, and the hatching grubs feed on the fruitlets around them. If you suspect the presence of raspberry beetle, spray with derris just as the fruits are beginning to change colour from green to pale pink. The derris will also kill off any lurking greenfly.

Red Berry, *see* **Blackberry Mite.**

Red core (*Phytophthora fragariae*) Only likely to occur in areas where drainage is poor. Gradually all plants infected will appear stunted and die. If you cut into the roots, they will appear red in the centre. Spores of the fungus can live in the soil for 12 years or more. See that the ground is properly drained (by correct soil preparation) before planting. If plants become infected, burn them; strawberries should not be planted on the infected land again.

Reversion 1 Used to describe the apparent return of the garden-raised cultivar to the wild or original plant. This can happen in two main ways: the swamping of the cultivar by the shoots of the original, as when a variegated plant produces green or reversion shoots, or when suckers from the rootstock of a grafted plant take over when the scion weakens or dies. **2** Also applied to a virus disease of blackcurrants that causes thin growth and smaller, fewer-lobed leaves, giving a 'wild' look to the plant.

Root death Caused by several species of *Phytophthora,* the same genus which causes potato blight. Areas of roots die and as a result shoots cease to grow and leaves are small and yellowish, wilting in warm weather. Total death usually follows. This disease is worst in moist and poorly drained soils particularly during warm weather. The chemical treatment available to nurseries cannot as yet be obtained by laymen gardeners. Improving drainage and avoiding the planting of trees and shrubs in infected sites is the only cure at the moment. Some of the most susceptible trees and shrubs are:- apple, beech, heathers, lime, ornamental plum and cherry, Lawson cypress and yew.

Above: one method of controlling rust fungus is by destroying the intermediate host, here the barberry.

Rose Leaf Rolling Sawfly, *see* Sawflies.

Rust Fungus Very small parasitic fungus, so called because of its rust-coloured spore masses. There are many different sorts, attacking a wide range of plants. They live within stem or leaf tissue as delicate hyphae and form flask- or cup-shaped fruiting bodies that burst open the tissue of the host plant to release their spores. Rust fungi have complicated life cycles. Some need two or more different kinds of host plants (heteroecious), eg Weymouth pine or five-needled pine rust (*Cronartium ribicola*), also on *Ribes* species; others live on one host (autoecious), eg mint rust (*Puccinia menthae*). At different times of the year they produce different kinds of spores. In summer, the usually pale brown or yellow, thin-walled uredospores are liberated. In autumn teleutospores, dark brown, thick-walled resting spores, are produced. After a period of dormancy these germinate to form a short, broad length of hyphae that bears basidiospores. The latter attack the host plant and in the spring produce the characteristic, cup-shaped structures called aecidial cups that bear the spring spores or aecidiospores. In the autoecious rusts all the stages are produced on the same host plant, but in the heteroecious sorts only one or two kinds of spores are borne on each of the various hosts. Most rust fungi are very damaging or weakening to the host plant, causing blotchy yellowing, premature leaf-fall and dieback of stems. In general, rusts are difficult to kill, but a fair degree of control can be obtained by using liquid or colloidal copper, mancozeb, maneb, thiram and zineb, used to makers' instructions. Mint rust can be controlled by warm water, treating the dormant rhizomes at 43·3°C (110°F) for 10 minutes, but care must be taken that the water temperature does not rise above 46°C (115°F). In agriculture and forestry, controls are obtained by eliminating the alternate – usually the winter – host plants, thus breaking a link in the rust's life cycle, eg destroying wild *Ribes* near five-needled pine plantations or *Berberis* near wheat fields.

Sawflies Large group of winged insects in the *Hymenoptera*, the order that also includes bees and wasps. The adult flies are not often recognized, but are easily distinguished from true flies by having four wings, and from bees by their lack of a waist, the abdomen and thorax running into each other, The larvae or grubs live on or within plants, and several species are well-known as garden pests. Those that feed on leaves superficially resemble the caterpillars of moths and butterflies, but have at least six pairs of false legs in the middle of the body, whereas true caterpillars have no more than four. Sawfly larvae are often conspicuous, feeding on the upper sides or edges of leaves, often with their 'tail' ends characteristically curled round and under. The less obvious and seldom seen larvae that tunnel into stems and fruit or that cause galls may lack prolegs entirely. The types of sawfly listed here are among the more obvious garden pests. **1** Apple (*Hoplocampa testudinea*), the larvae of which attack very young fruit that soon falls; sometimes confused with codlin moth (qv) that appears later and attacks larger fruit. **2** Gooseberry (*Nematus ribesii*), whose young larvae, having black heads and black-dotted, green bodies feed communally on leaves; when larger they disperse and feed singly, losing the black dots. **3** Plum (*Hoplocampa flava*), a close ally of the apple sawfly, the larvae attacking young plum fruit with similar results. **4** Rose leaf rolling (*Blennocampa pusilla*), whose larvae roll rose leaflets into the characteristic tight cylinders, feeding in the middle. **5** Solomon's seal (*Phymatocera aterrima*), whose larvae feed communally on the leaves, a severe attack leading to complete defoliation. Control of those species that have easily seen larvae is readily effected by hand-picking or spraying with derris of malathion. Larvae within rolled leaves are also best hand-picked but can be sprayed with HCH (BHC) and trichlorphon, particularly from early summer onwards as a preventative. Larvae in fruit cannot be directly controlled once the attack has started, and a preventative spraying with malathion or HCH (BHC) immediately after petal-fall is the best measure coupled with raking up and burning windfall fruit at frequent intervals.

Scab General term for the damage done to leaves stems, fruit and roots by certain fungi. These attack the surface tissue, causing irregular, blackish to brownish, scab-like areas. Scab diseases are seldom lethal but spoil the effect and value of the plants parts they attack. Apple and pear scab (*Venturia*) is widespread, disfiguring the fruit and leaves with sooty to brownish-green blotches and cracks; it also damages the young shoots, causing blisters and cracks. Infected trees should be regularly mulched with organic matter and all damaged shoots cut out.

Above: scab on potatoes is rarely lethal, only superficially disfiguring.

Scale insects Although allied to capsid bugs, these insects resemble tiny limpets and are totally sedentary once the juvenile (nymphal) stage is completed. About a dozen species occur on cultivated plants; in shape they are typified by brown scale and mussel scale. Brown scale is almost hemispherical in outline, brown and glossy. Mussel scale is like a mussel shell in shape, brown and flattish.

All scale insects are active when young. The young nymphs are known as crawlers because of the way in which the insects spread around. Systemic insecticides such as dimethoate and formathion usually kill the adult scales. The best way to tackle these insects outside is to spray with malathion, nicotine or diazinon while the crawlers are active during late spring and early summer.

Sciarid flies Often called mushroom flies, these are tiny true flies, usually under 6mm ($\frac{1}{4}$ in) long, the larvae (grubs) of which feed on dead organic matter, mushrooms and other fungi and sometimes on small seedlings. In the greenhouse, or where long-term seed pans are kept, these tiny flies can be recognised by the way they run across the soil with wings vibrating. Over-moist soil conditions attract them. The cylindrical larvae tunnel just under the surface and may feed on germinating seeds or seedling stems and roots. When on mushrooms, their tunnelling and feeding activities spoil the crop. Malathion, HCH, nicotine and dichlovos are all efficient control substances.

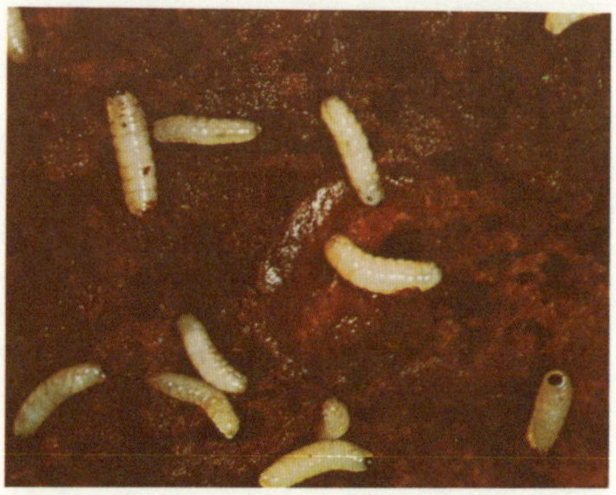

Above: larvae of sciarid flies which are attracted by over-moist soils.

Shanking Applied primarily to a physiological disorder of grapes that results in a shrivelling and browning of the developing berries. It appears to be caused by an irregular water supply or lack of essential nutrients. In subsequent years mulch and feed as recommended and make sure the plants never lack water. If necessary use a soil auger or dig a narrow test hole close to the root system to make sure the soil is moist down to at least 45cm (18 in).

Silver leaf (*Chondrostereum purpureum*) Common disease of trees which has a preference for members of the rose family (*Rosaceae*), eg plum, cherry, apple, pear, apricot and hawthorn. In its early stages, when only a few leaves are silvered, it can often be controlled by cutting away all the silvered shoots down to clean, unstained wood. A heavily-silvered tree, however, will rarely survive. The silvered leaves are not infectious, but in time the wood bearing them dies, and fungal infections appear on it. These discharge masses of spores that endanger not only plums but other fruit in the garden as well. In the final stage of silvering the leaves are very torn, with brown edges and brown-edged holes. Branch breakage under heavy crops is a frequent cause of silver leaf. To prevent this, thin the small fruits in mid summer (June) to one per cluster. Excessive crops will not produce high-quality fruit, so thinning is often needed anyway. Where branches remain heavily laden even after thinning, prop them up with stout forked sticks, with a pad in the fork to prevent chafing. Never let wall ties bite into the wood of fans, and always allow sufficient room for shoot and branch expansion. If any branches get damaged, remove them at once and paint the wounds immediately with grafting wax or horticultural bitumen paint. It is useless to take these protective measures long after the damage has occurred; if silver leaf is going to infect it will do so at the time of the damage or very soon afterwards. If treatment is left until too late and the wood is already infected, the disease will be sealed in.

Slugs and Snails These familiar pests are members of the animal phylum *Mollusca* and class *Gastropoda*. Their slimy bodies lack legs and move forwards by a rippling motion of the under-surface or 'stomach'. The main point of difference between slugs and snails is the possession of a shell. This is not a clear-cut distinction, however, as some slugs have rudimentary shells, although these are generally hidden by a fold or mantle of body tissue. An exception to this is the shelled slug (*Testacella haliotidea*), a carnivorous species feeding on worms, other slugs and soil creatures. It is 8–12cm (3–5 in) long when fully extended, dull greyish-yellow, with an oval 7 × 5 mm ($\frac{1}{4} \times \frac{1}{5}$ in) shell at the tail. The most destructive plant-feeding slugs are: **1** large black (*Arion ater*), extending to 15cm (6 in) long and varying in colour from black to brick red or brown; **2** netted or grey (*Agriolimax*

Below: a field slug (Deroceras reticulatum).

Above: the pearly white eggs of the field slug are most likely to be laid in loose soil, bark or other decaying vegetation. Top: two garden slugs (Arion hortensis), *hollowing their way through a strawberry.*

Above: snails can be attracted away from seedlings by leaving decaying plants around. Top: the courtship dance of two Roman snails.

reticulatus), extending to 3·5cm (1½ in) long, whitish to brownish-yellow with a pattern of brown grooves, spots and streaks, sometimes totally blue-black; **3** smooth jet (*Milax gagates*), extending to 5cm (2 in) long, grey or black with the body keeled above; largely subterranean and feeding in a variety of root crops, particularly potatoes. Of similar habits to these three is Sowerby's slug (*M. sowerbyi*), to 7cm (2¾ in) long, pale to dark brown or grey with darker specks and a pale keel. The commonest and most damaging of the garden snails is the common or garden snail (*Helix aspersa*) with a rounded shell up to 3·5cm (1½ in) wide, buff or yellowish, boldly banded dark brown. Complete eradication of slugs and snails is not possible but proprietary slug killers with metaldehyde or methiocarb (Draza) base with thin them out. Traps of orange or grapefruit skins, lettuce or cabbage leaves may be left where damage occurs, visited daily and slugs and snails destroyed. In addition, hiding places such as heaps of bricks, tiles, wood etc, should be searched regularly.

Slugworms Vernacular name for the larvae of certain sawflies (qv) that are slimy above and resemble small slugs. Two species are sometimes troublesome in gardens: **1** pear and cherry slugworm (*Eriocampa limacina*). The larva is deep olive to blackish-green, somewhat humped at the head end to appear more realistically slug-like. It feeds on pear, cherry, plum, apple, quince and species of *Chaenomeles*, grazing always the upper leaf surface and leaving unsightly, brownish, skeletonized patches. More often, or obviously, seen is: **2** rose slugworm (*Endelomyia aethiops*). The larva is slug-like, pale greenish-yellow, but lacks a slimy coating. It damages the upper leaf surface in the same way as the pear slugworm. Both slugworms can be controlled by hand-picking if the attack is slight, or by spraying with derris or HCH (BHC).

Smuts These are fungal diseases closely allied to the rusts qv and in some cases similar to look at, but producing blackish spores. Few are common or serious, the most unsightly sorts being those which attack flowers. The worst of these is carnation anther smut (*Ustilago violacea*) which stunts flower heads and causes deformed anthers which burst into a mass of messy, sooty spores. This disease is systemic, so infected plants are best destroyed. However, a choice or rare cultivar can sometimes be cured by spraying weekly with maneb, thiram or zineb.

Sodium Among the most widespread of all elements and present in every soil. It is not essential for plant growth, either as a major or minor (trace element) mineral nutrient. However, it is beneficial for some plants, eg beetroot, sugar beet, and perhaps others, too.

Soft rot Descriptive of the way plant tissues are reduced to a foul-smelling brown mush by certain bacteria and fungi. Most examples of soft rot are caused by the bacterium *Erwinia carotovora*. It mainly attacks bulbs and root vegetables, usually those that have been grown too soft or damaged by tools or pests. Badly drained soil conditions aggravate infection. Destroying attacked plants, improving soil drainage and avoiding over-use of nitrogenous fertilizers are the only ways of minimizing this trouble.

Above: leaves afflicted with sooty mould, a fungi that is unsightly but not lethal.

Solomon's-Seal Sawfly, *see* Sawflies.

Sooty mould Minute fungi that colonize the sweet sticky exudations (honeydew) from aphids. Although they render leaves, stems and sometimes flowers unsightly and cut down the amount of light received by the plant, they are not parasitic. The only control is to eliminate the aphids, qv.

Spider-mite Microscopic member of the order *Acarina* (true mites). Spider-mites are related to spiders and basically resemble them when viewed under a lens. Unlike true spiders, however, they have unsegmented bodies and live by sucking plant sap. Young mites have six legs, only developing the full complement of eight at maturity. Three spider-mites and their closely related species can be serious pests in the garden. **1** Gooseberry red spider (*Bryobia* species): these are the largest of the common spider-mites and can be seen with the naked eye, appearing as reddish specks, fast-moving, in warm, sunny weather. They attack a wide variety of plants, particularly apple, gooseberry and ivy, plus many weeds and grass. Attack symptoms show first as a light mottling on the upper leaf sur-

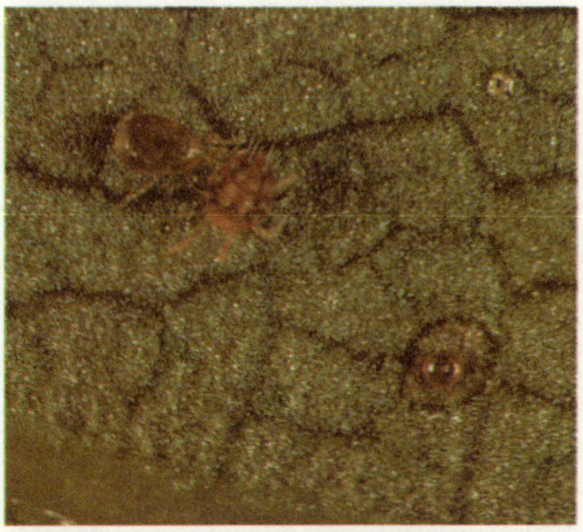

Above: a pear-shaped predatory mite attacks a pest red spider mite.

Above: lettuce stem rotted through by grey mould (botrytis).

Above: caterpillar of the common or garden swiftmoth (Hepialus lupulina).

faces; later the leaf bronzes over and then withers. At the first signs of damage, spray with dimethoate, formathion or malathion. **2** Fruit tree red spider (*Panonychus ulmi*): these reddish mites are microscopic, normally tree-dwelling and sometimes serious pests on apples and plums causing mottling, bronzing and premature leaf-fall. They are usually most prevalent on trees that are regularly sprayed with DNOC winter wash, which kills the natural predators. Spray with malathion or formathion only when necessary and after the petals have fallen. The fungicide dinocap, used to control mildew, also gives some spider control. **3** Glasshouse or greenhouse red spider (*Tetranychus urticae* and allies): these are microscopic and similar to fruit tree red spider, varying from almost colourless to variously spotted or flushed red. Damage is also leaf-mottling, withering and leaf-fall, and severe infestations may show as a light webbing over leaves and shoot-tips. They are exceedingly troublesome in greenhouses, particularly under hot, dry conditions, but they also attack plants outside in summer, especially those trained on sheltered walls. Regular damping down and syringing the plants sometimes checks – but never eliminates – them. Fumigating greenhouses with azobenzene to maker's instructions can be recommended, and also spraying with the substances mentioned above, plus liquid derris. Never use the same insecticide twice running as glasshouse red spider-mites are quick to build up resistant strains. Biological control is now coming into its own, using the predatory mite *Phytoseiulus persimilis* from Chile. Fellows of the RHS can obtain it from Wisley Gardens.

Split fruits and root vegetables Caused by letting the plants get dry and then watering heavily. Fruits and root vegetables cannot absorb the water fast enough and the skin ruptures. It ought not to occur in a greenhouse where watering can be controlled, but it is sometimes difficult to prevent outdoors when periods of drought are followed by heavy rains unless you water regularly during dry spells.

Spur blight, *see* Brown Rot.

Stem rots Many annual, perennial and some shrubby plants may develop zones of rotting, resulting in wilting of leaves and then usually toppling of the stem above the attack. Grey mould (*Botrytis)* qv is often the culprit, but other fungi and bacteria can be the cause. The soft wet rot is often caused by the bacterium *Erwinia carotovora* and for this there is no reliable chemical cure. All diseased tissue must be cut out and the plant kept as dry as possible. Dusting with copper/lime dust often helps. Other stem roots should be treated similarly, spraying with captan, benomyl, dichlofluanid or thiram, one of which should be effective.

Sulphur Major nutrient element usually present in soils as sulphates combined with other minerals, eg calcium, potassium, sodium. Sulphur is essential for the proper growth of plants, being a constituent of protoplasm and proteins. Deficiency symptoms are similar to those of nitrogen deficiency, leaves being very pale green and smaller than usual, in some species taking on bright tints. A dressing of superphosphate or sulphate of ammonia is an effective remedy. Sulphur in a powdered form used as a dust, or in a colloidal form as a spray, is a useful fungicide against powdery mildew, apple and pear scab and big-bud mite of blackcurrants. It also checks spider mites. However, some plants can be damaged by sulphur sprays and are known as sulphur-shy, eg, red- and whitecurrants, and such cultivars of apple as Beauty of Bath, Cox's Orange Pippin, and Rival.

Sun scald Plants suddenly exposed to hot sunlight can be damaged, the surface skin and tissue partially 'cooking'. Damage shows as pale brown patches or slightly sunken or papery areas on fruits, eg grape, tomato, gooseberry and on the soft bark of cherry, maple and beech. Leaves may look as if scorched. Damage is usually to plants under glass or to those where a screen of other plants or a fence, is removed in summer. Damaged fruit and foliage are best removed to prevent them from being attacked by such fungi as grey mould.

Swift moth Caterpillar of several species of hepialid moths, living and feeding permanently well below soil level and therefore differing from cutworms (qv). It is further distinguished by being whitish or creamy in colour and capable of wriggling backwards and forwards when disturbed. Although seldom a real pest in gardens, it can feed on a wide range of herbaceous perennials, including rhubarb and such weeds as nettles, and in quantity may severely weaken the root systems. Most likely to be seen is the common or garden swift (*Hepialus lupulina*), which may feed on gladioli corms, potatoes and iris rhizomes. In severe infestations the plants are best dug up, freed of soil and caterpillars, and replanted in clean soil to recover. Apply HCH (BHC) dust to the surrounding area and fork in.

Tarsonemid mites The mite family *Tarsonemidae* contains many microscopic pests which feed in buds, in shoot tips, under leaf sheaths and in bulbs. By feeding on very young shoot tips and buds, they check the growth of the plant, and the leaves and stems that do expand are badly crippled and show a light brown scarring. Flower buds may be killed or malformed. Damage is more noticeable under glass. There is no really efficient chemical cure, though dusting plants with powdered sulphur does check or stop the attack if used while temperatures are above 18°C (64°F). Heat treatment is effective but tricky to do efficiently without proper equipment. Infected plants are totally immersed in water maintained at a steady 46°C (115°F) for 7 minutes. See also Bulb mites.

Tar Spot, *see* Leaf Blotches.

Thrips Minute sap-sucking creature also known as thunder-fly; member of the insect order *Thyrsanoptera* (fringed wings). Adult thrips are very slender, rarely more than 3mm ($\frac{1}{8}$ in) long, usually black or brown, sometimes yellowish, with two pairs of wings that are responsible for the name of the order to which they belong, being little more than flattened bristles fringed with long, stiff hairs. Many thrips inhabit flowers and in small numbers do little damage. In large numbers, however, they can be a serious pest, causing a pale or silvery mottling and a stunting or malformation of shoot-tips, flower-buds and young fruit. Among plants particularly prone to thrips damage are: calceolarias, garden peas, gladioli, onions, *Sinningia, Zantedeschia.* Apart from the physical damage, thrips also transmit viruses from infected to clean plants. At the first signs of damage spray with derris, HCH (BHC) or malathion.

Tomato leaf curl When the leaves curl upwards this is generally a sign that the plants are receiving too much nitrogen. Occasionally it may be caused by minute quantities of spray from a selective weed-killer. Tomatoes are especially vulnerable to these and the greatest care must be taken when using them anywhere near tomato plants.

Tortrix moths The adult tortrix moths are seldom seen or recognized by gardeners. There are several species, some with caterpillars that eat only leaves and others that also feed on or in young fruits of apple, pear, plum and cherry. This latter group is the most damaging in gardens. Adult moths lay eggs singly. After hatching the caterpillars start by eating the leaves, which they tie together with silken threads. As they get larger they transfer their attentions to the fruit itself, scarring the skin with small pits. The damage to the fruit is superficial, and the apples are perfectly good to eat after peeling. The trouble is that the scarring renders the fruit useless for keeping, and it has to be eaten fresh off the tree. Spray with fenitrothion in mid-June and again two weeks later. This is not a total cure but will prevent most fruit damage.

Below: foliage attacked by thrips which can also transmit viruses from infected to clean plants.

Tulip fire (*Botrytis tulipae*) The most damaging of tulip diseases, particularly during cold, wet springs. It starts on leaves and petals as dark spots and streaks that soon turn brown. Leaf tips may blacken as if scorched and stems rot at leaf-axils, causing toppling at that point. Infection of the bulb shows as a grey mould and small, black, resting bodies by which the fungus can persist in the soil. Attacked plants should be destroyed and the remainder sprayed with maneb, thiram (Ferna-Col) or zineb. When lifted, the bulbs should be dusted with quintozene (Botrilex). If the site is to be used for tulips again, dress the soil with the latter fungicide and rake in. When young shoots are 3–5cm (1–2 in) tall spray with maneb, etc, repeating at 10-day intervals until flowering.

Violet root rot (*Helicobasidium purpureum*) Affects several plant groups and is easily recognized by the characteristic strands of purple mycelium on the plant roots. Destroy all infected plants and introduce resistant crops. Violet root rot only rarely occurs in land that is in good heart and so attention to drainage and soil fertility is the best means of prevention.

Walnut bacterial blight (*Pseudomonas juglandis*) Produces small black spots on the leaves and black, sunken, watery-looking areas on the husks of the nuts. A severe attack can ruin the crop. The bacteria overwinter in black lesions on one-year shoots, and in bud scales. To treat, cut out all such shoots in winter, and after a heavy infection, spray with a liquid copper fungicide soon after the tree has leafed out, but before the flowers appear. Repeat again immediately after the tree has flowered. This blight is spread by summer rain. In districts where the disease is persistent it may be necessary to spray on a routine basis in mid and late summer (mid June and mid July).

Wart disease (*Synchytrium endobioticum*). Soil-dwelling fungus disease of potato tubers. Infected tubers often bear large, warty or cauliflower-like outgrowths, and later rot and disintegrate. Resting or dormant spores are released and infect young tubers the following year. This is a notifiable disease and if found in Britain must be reported to the Ministry of Agriculture, Fisheries and Food. All the newer potato cultivars are bred for immunity to the disease but some of the old ones are susceptible. There is no cure and potatoes must not be grown in infected land.

Above: a parasitic wasp Encarsia formosa *attacking a whitefly nymph.*

Weevil Member of the beetle family CURCULIONIDAE, typified by the presence of a snout or rostrum that bears the jaws and antennae, Practically all of the 40,000 known species of weevils (500 of them British) are plant feeders and a few are pests of garden plants. It is the juvenile phase of the weevil's life cycle that is most damaging, the legless, whitish larvae or grubs tunnelling into – and feeding on – buds, stems, roots and seed. Only the vine weevil (*Otiorhynchus sulcatus*), the similar and closely related clay-coloured weevil (*O. singularis*) and the pea and bean weevil (*Sitona lineatus*), are likely to be a real nuisance in the garden or greenhouse. The first two are large as weevils go, to 8mm ($\frac{1}{3}$in) or more long, usually blackish or brownish. The adult insects feed on a variety of plants, either making small holes or notching the edges of thicker leaves, eg rhododendron, cyclamen, various ferns, peach, raspberry, strawberry and grape-vine. The larval stage is spent underground in roots and corms, being commonest on primulas, cyclamen, begonias, saxifrages and other alpines. Control comprises a combination of good garden hygiene, particularly in the greenhouse, removal of debris where the adults hide by day, and the use of HCH (BHC) dust added to the compost of susceptible pot plants at potting time or brushed on leaves and stems where signs of feeding are seen. Pea and bean weevil is about 6mm ($\frac{1}{2}$ in) long, brownish-yellow with darker, longitudinal stripes and a short, thick snout. It feeds on the leaves of peas, beans and other members of the same family (*Leguminosae*), eating notches out of leaf margins rendering them unsightly. The larvae (grubs) feed on the root nodules of the same plants. Dusting the leaves and seedlings of young plants with HCH or derris is an effective control treatment.

White blisters Although widespread diseases, these allies of the downy mildews are seldom serious. The commonest sort is crucifer white blister which attacks members of the cabbage family (*Cruciferae*). It starts with small white lesions on the leaves which become powdery with spores. When spores are produced in quantity, the leaves look as if splashed with white paint. Leaves and stems become deformed. Heavily infected plants should be destroyed, the remainder sprayed with Bordeaux mixture.

Whitefly Tiny member of the insect order *Hemiptera* (true bugs) and allied to the aphid. It is easily identified by its waxy-white colouring and moth-like shape, even though only about 1·25mm ($\frac{1}{20}$ in) long. It is a sap-sucker and large numbers can cause a yellow mottling of the foliage and a general weakening of the plant. Like the aphid it also secretes honeydew that encourages unsightly sooty mounds. Its life cycle is spent on leaf undersides and differs somewhat from that of most bugs. The eggs are laid in circular groups and hatch into mobile, wingless nymphs or larvae. The larva then settles down, changes its skin and becomes immobile and scale-like. When fully grown it stops feeding and enters a resting or dormant phase similar to the pupal or chrysalid stage of moths and beetles, from which the adult whitefly eventually emerges. About 1000 species are known throughout the world, several of these in Britain and USA. Most important is the greenhouse whitefly (*Trialeurodes vaporariorum*), which

Left: pea and bean weevils bite semi-circular notches.

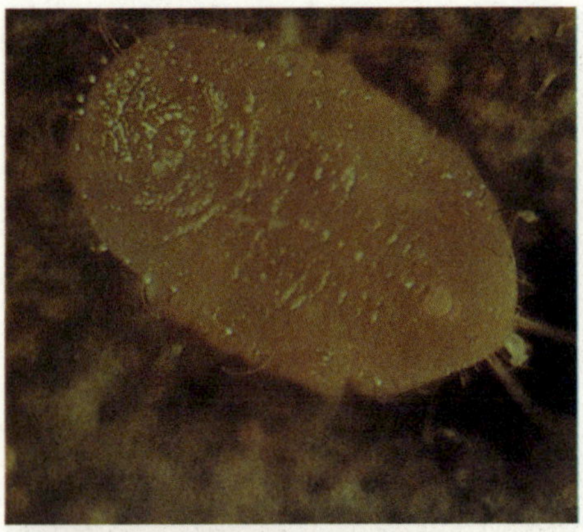

Above left: a mobile whitefly nymph or 'scale'. These hatch out from the eggs laid by the adult female whitefly on the underside of leaves, and move off to suitable feeding places, where they settle down. These small almost transparent bodies are difficult to see. Above centre: whitefly larvae, or nymphs, which have been parasitized by the wasp Encarsia formosa, *turn black. Above right: whitefly larvae, some of which have been parasitized. Right: sooty moulds often develop after whitefly infestation. Far right: adult whiteflies sucking sap from leaves.*

attacks a wide range of plants, particularly abutilon, begonia, calceolaria, chrysanthemum, cineraria, heliotrope, tomato and cucumber. Also abundant is the cabbage whitefly (*Aleyrodes proletella*), which attacks all brassicas and several allied plants. Other species are found on rhododendron, lonicera, phillyrea and viburnum. Control is not easy, but possible.

CHEMICAL CONTROL It is not easy to control whitefly with pesticides because most insecticides are only effective against the adults – the eggs, nymphs and pupae being resistant. This poses particular problems, especially in the case of greenhouse and cabbage whitefly, where continuous breeding results in the constant presence of the resistant developmental stages. Consequently, an extended programme of insecticidal treatments at fortnightly intervals is necessary in order to obtain reasonable control of these troublesome pests.

Fortunately the chemical control of whitefly has been improved by the recent introduction of resmethrin, bioresmethrin and pirimiphos-methyl, which are active against the developmental stages as well as against the adults. Using these insecticides, it is now possible to obtain effective control of these difficult pests with a simple programme of three treatments at three to four day intervals.

For the control of outdoor species, the insecticide can be applied either as a spray or by aerosol. These two methods can also be used indoors but, in addition, it is possible to use HCH (BHC) smoke generators in the greenhouse. Whatever, the method of application, however, it is important to check whether or not the selected chemical is safe for use on the infested plants. Cucumbers, for instance, are sensitive to many pesticidal formulas, as are cacti, succulents, ferns and orchids. In the case of edible crops such as tomatoes, melons, cucumbers and brassicas, it is also essential to note the minimal recommended interval between treatment and harvesting the crop to avoid any danger of poisoning.

BIOLOGICAL CONTROL An alternative approach to the control of greenhouse whitefly is the use of the parasitic wasp *Encarsia formosa,* which destroys the nymphs. This is a tiny, winged insect that is only the size of a small pin-head, yet the female can lay sufficient eggs in a fortnight to parasitize 50 whitefly nymphs. A single egg is laid in each nymph and about ten days after the egg hatches, the parasitized nymph turns black and so is easily recognizable. Altogether it takes about a month after the eggs are laid before a fresh generation of adult parasites emerges to begin a new cycle.

Temperature is very important in the life of this parasite and in practice a minimum temperature of 13°C (55°F) is needed for it to operate efficiently. As a result, this method of control is only suitable for use in well-heated greenhouses. Poor light also reduces the activity of the wasp, thus limiting its period of usefulness to between early summer and early autumn (May and August). Another limitation is that *E. formosa* is averse to attacking nymphs on plants with sticky or aromatic leaves. So it is not very effective against whitefly on nicotiana and scented-leaved pelargoniums. Another problem involved in the use of this helpful insect is that it is sensitive to most insecticides. Consequently it is not generally possible to control other greenhouse pests at the same time.

INTEGRATED CONTROL The use of 'integrated control', referring to biological control combined with carefully-selected chemical treatments, is still in its infancy. One simple example is the use of pirimicarb to control aphids in greenhouses where whitefly are being controlled by *E. formosa*. This is possible because pirimicarb, whilst giving excellent control of greenfly, has no ill effects on the parasitic wasp. This system can be elaborated by the use of the predatory mite, *Phytoseiulus persimilis*, to control red spider mites. Other pests can be controlled with soil drenches of systemic chemicals and by the use of short-persistent pesticides prior to the introduction of the parasites or predators. Much research is, however, still needed before integrated pest control can be regarded as normal practice.

White Rot (*Sclerotium cepivorum*) Fungal disease of onions, leeks, garlic, shallots, mainly affecting seedlings and young plants. Plants stop growing, the leaves turn yellow and the young bulb becomes covered with a mesh of white hyphae and then rots. This disease is more likely to occur among crowded plants and during warm summers. It overwinters as small, black, resting bodies

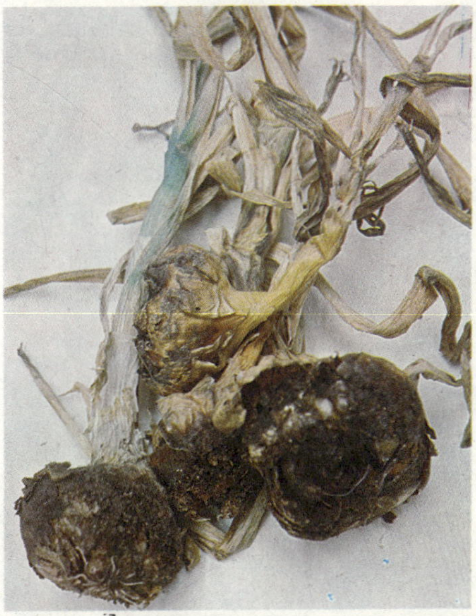

known as sclerotia, that – in the absence of new seedlings – can remain viable in the soil for up to 8 years. Infected plants should be destroyed and a new site chosen for subsequent crops. If onions must be grown on the same land again, the seed drills must be dressed with benomyl, calomel or thiophanate-methyl. The best control substance is iprodione but at present it is only available to commercial growers.

White Rust *(Puccinia horiana)* Serious disease of chrysanthemums, the first symptoms being yellow blotches on the upper leaf surfaces that become more pronounced, then develop brown centres. Pustules appear on the leaf undersides that are at first waxy-buff or pinkish, then turn white as the teleutospores develop (see Rust fungus). There is no cure and plants must be destroyed. It is a notifiable disease and any outbreak in Britain must be reported to the Ministry of Agriculture, Fisheries and Food.

Wireworm Larva or grub stage of many species of click beetles or skipjacks belonging to the insect order *Coleoptera*, family ELATERIDAE. It is a more or less cylindrical, tough-skinned, yellow or yellow-brown creature, to 2.5cm (1 in) or more long, that feeds underground on plant roots. It is primarily an inhabitant of grassland and usually only a pest when fields are turned into gardens. It can be very damaging in the vegetable garden, particularly to root crops. The adult beetle is 1–2cm ($\frac{2}{5}$-$\frac{4}{5}$ in) long, slender, almost elliptical. When disturbed it feigns death, but if turned over on its back it straightens suddenly with a click and flips over, landing on its feet. Frequent cultivation of the soil will reduce the number of wireworms, allowing birds to get them more easily, and all specimens should be destroyed. Severely infested soil should be dressed with HCH (BHC) dust, but it may taint some root vegetables.

Above: a wireworm – the larva or grub stage of many species of click beetle – feeds underground on plant roots. It can be very damaging in the vegetable garden, particularly to root crops. Left: onions affected with white rot.

Witches' broom Often very dense, sometimes birch-broom-like mass of twigs that occurs on many kinds of trees, especially birch, elm, pine and other conifers. Witches' brooms are variously caused by fungi, the feeding of mites, or mutation. Plants propagated from mutational brooms often stay dwarf and this is the origin of many pigmy conifer cultivars.

Wither Tip, *see* Brown Rot.

Woodlice Small, oval creatures, characterized by a series of overlapping oblong plates down the back and about 14 legs, which are all too familiar to most gardeners. There are several species, three being fairly common including the pill woodlouse which rolls into a ball when alarmed. They feed on organic matter, mostly decayed plant remains, but seedlings, roots and fruits are sometimes gnawed. Feeding takes place at night. The main way of getting rid of them is to remove the damp rubbish and litter beneath which they hide by day. Infestations can be dealt with by putting down such bait as bran, boiled potato or dried blood mixed with HCH or carbaryl.

Below: two types of woodlice, Oniscus ascellus *and a pair of the lighter coloured* Porcellio scaber.

A-Z ORNAMENTAL PLANTS ATTACKED

Acer (maples) Acers are relatively free from disease, but are attacked by aphids and red spider mites; Japanese maples growing in a warm position are particularly prone to this.

Althaea, Alcea (hollyhock) Hollyhocks are remarkably trouble free but for the one major disease, rust. However, if plants are grown as annuals or biennials and always raised regularly from seed, rust is less likely to occur or be severe.

Annuals (hardy and half-hardy) If annuals are to provide a long and colourful display it is necessary to eliminate the worst pests and diseases at an early stage. Happily, there are not very many to worry about. In the seedling stage, damping off disease may occur. Later, aphids and capsid bugs can be major pests. Earwigs, froghoppers, slugs and snails are other pests to watch out for. Mildew and botrytis (grey mould) are diseases that may be a nuisance.

Antirrhinum (snapdragon) The greatest enemy of antirrhinums used to be rust, but today there are many cultivars which are rust-resistant and so-labelled on the packet. It is worth paying a little extra for better quality, especially as the seed goes such a long way.
See also comments under Annuals.

Aster (Chinese), *see Callistephus.*

Azalea Botanically, the azaleas are members of the large genus *Rhododendron* (qv). They are, however, more prone to certain pests and diseases.

Whitefly particularly infest azaleas. Azalea gall causes the young leaves and flowers, particularly of the kurumes, to form small swellings that are red or pale green, then white and eventually brown.

Begonia Tuberous begonias in pots may suffer vine weevil damage to the tuber and roots. Tarsonemid mite can cripple foliage and flowers of both tuberous and fibrous rooted plants. All begonias both

Opposite: a colourful summer border. Far left: the leaves of Acer pseudoplatanus Brilliantissimum. *Left:* Althaea rosea. *Above:* Begonia semperflorens.

under glass and outside can be attacked by aphids, whitefly and affected by powdery mildew.

Berberis (barberry) Berberis are fairly free from pests, nor are they very prone to disease but they are sometimes attacked by barberry rust and honey fungus. Rust disease sometimes occurs.

Bulbs, corms, tubers Both hardy bulbs and those needing greenhouse or home culture are remarkably free of pests and diseases. On occasions though, several pests can be troublesome. Narcissus fly, both the large and small species, attack daffodils, narcissi, hyacinth, snowdrop and some other sorts. Tarsonemid mites can be serious on a wide range of greenhouse bulbous, cormous, tuberous and rhizomatous plants. Bulb mites can further the damage. In some areas, stem eelworm can ruin narcissus, daffodils, hyacinths, snowdrops, tulips and scillas. Other pests include aphids, slugs, vine weevil and wireworm. Bulbs, corms and tubers in store may develop blue mould disease.

Cacti and other succulents In general, all the succulent plants including the members of the cactus family (*Cactaceae*) are remarkably free of diseases and pests. Neglected collections of these plants are often attacked by root and stem mealy bugs, red spider mite, white fly and scale insects. Less bothersome are aphids, slugs and snails. Overwatered and overfed specimens may contract stem rot disease.

Callistephus (China aster) Unlike most popular annuals, the China aster is particularly prone to wilt disease, though much depends on the season and the way the plants are treated during the hardening off period. There are now a few wilt resistant cultivars, eg the mixed-coloured 'Earliest of All'.

Calluna (heather) Until comparatively recently, it could have been said of heaths and heathers that they had no real pest and disease troubles. Root death *(Phytophthora)* is now a widespread disease and can be serious. Rabbits are occasionally a pest and lime induced chlorosis (iron deficiency) occurs where there is free lime in the soil.

Above: Camellias are susceptible to soft scale, mealy bugs and vine weevils.

Camellia Both under glass and outside in warm sites, soft scale is an important pest of camellias. Under glass, mealy bug and vine weevil can be nuisances. Where there is too much lime, iron deficiency will occur. Frost will brown expanding buds and blooms.

Carnation, *see* Dianthus.

Chrysanthemum Major and less serious pests are numerous, some of the more important being: aphids, earwigs, capsid bugs, thrips, leaf miner and, under glass, red spider mite and whitefly. As the weather warms up, the pests begin to multiply. Start a routine preventative spraying programme after planting to keep your plants pest-free. Use nicotine sprays when the weather is warm, but change to malathion or a mixture of gamma HCH (BHC) and menazon in cooler conditions. Pirimicarb is also very effective. It is advisable to alternate the available pesticides since some pests appear to build up an immunity if just one is used continuously. Among diseases, powdery mildew, ray blight and grey mould are likely, especially late in the season.

Below: Calluna *(heather) may be attacked by root death* (Phytaphthora).

Above: remarkably trouble-free, clematis can nevertheless fall prey to wilt.

Clematis Although wilt can be serious in some areas and mildew, aphids, earwigs, slugs and snails do at least a little damage each year, the many species and cultivars of clematis are remarkably trouble-free plants, provided their basic growing requirements are met.

Climbing plants Most hardy climbing plants are seldom seriously attacked by pests and diseases. In the open garden, aphids and earwigs are the greatest nuisances. Plants growing through trees may get covered with sooty mould. On walls, scale insects may appear. Under glass, red spider mite and whitefly are the most generally serious. Mealy bug can also be a pest of warm greenhouses. Drought symptoms can be experienced both inside and out.

Conifers Conifers are generally free from both pests and diseases, but most plants have their enemies and there are a few that can attack certain species and varieties. Red spider mite will attack picea – particularly *Picea glauca albertiana* Conica (Alberta spruce), and varieties of chamaecyparis and juniperus. These attacks come during dry, hot periods, and plants should be sprayed two or three times in the summer with a systemic insecticide. It should be done in the evening when foliage is dry and not too hot. In some areas, honey fungus and root death (*Phytophthora*) are serious diseases.

Above: Chamaecyparis lawsoniana *Fletcherii.*

Above: the crocus flower is often attacked by birds.

Above: Dahlias seem to be particularly attractive to pests.

Cotoneaster Apart from the possibility of being infested with greenfly and scale insects in the summer, cotoneasters are fairly free from pests. Possibly the most frustrating are birds, which steal their berries in wintertime. Being members of the ROSACEAE family, cotoneasters are subject to possible infection with fireblight, which blackens the flowers and kills the branches. Other diseases that might possibly affect them are honey fungus disease and silverleaf.

Crab-apple, *see* Malus.

Crataegus (Hawthorn) The most troublesome pests are caterpillars, and these should be picked off as they appear. If the infestation is serious, spray with a systemic insecticide such as fenitrothion. In common with other members of the ROSACEAE family, crataegus are subject to fireblight that blackens and shrivels the flowers and causes the branches to die back and the leaves to turn brown and wither. Honey fungus is another disease that is fatal to crataegus and powdery mildew is a less deadly disease that can attack. Yet another fungus disease is silver leaf.

Crocus Although all the gladiolus corm diseases and both grey and blue mould can attack crocuses, birds pecking the flowers and mice eating the corms are usually the two most irritating troubles.

Cyclamen Hardy cyclamen, particularly *C.hederifolium* (*neapolitanum*), are largely pest and disease free. Pot grown specimens under glass or in the home may suffer from grey mould, powdery mildew, wilt, leaf spots, bacterial soft rot, root rot and vine weevil.

Above: Cyclamen are largely pest free.

Dahlia The slow-moving blackfly and the greenfly are an easy target for a high-pressure sprayer, and if you choose to launch a regular attack – say once every ten days during the summer months – with an insecticide based on malathion, derris or BHC, then you should never see any of these aphids on your dahlias.

Thrips and capsids are fairly fast-moving, and not easily eliminated with a contact spray. But if you occasionally use one of the systemic insecticides where the chemical is taken into the cellular structure of the plant, then even these persistent invaders will be kept away.

Slugs and snails can be troublesome on occasions, especially in the young plant stage, when on a warm midsummer evening they can do a great deal of damage in a very short time.

As for earwigs, the dahlia is no more a special home for these pests than any other garden flower. It is true, of course, that its speed and scaly surface make the earwig difficult to control, but a regular programme of spraying generally will not only eliminate those that venture onto your plants, but deter others from making their home in the leaf and bud. If you are particularly troubled with earwigs, then the root cause may be that you are providing cover for breeding in other parts of the garden. Loose bark on trellis, overgrown shrubs and bushes, decaying wood or areas of tufted grass make excellent homes for young earwig families. A well-tried method of control that has been with dahlia growers for a century or more is to trap them.

Control of insect attack is always a matter of importance, whether your dahlias are in the greenhouse at propagating time or in full bloom in early autumn (August). Insects, especially the sap-sucking varieties, spread virus disease by transferring infected sap from a virused dahlia to a healthy plant; once the parasites get the upper hand, it would not take too long for a whole collection to be damaged permanently.

Delphinium Delphiniums do not attract the attention of many of the common garden pests. Both aphids and caterpillars leave them alone. Their principal enemies are the slug and the snail. Although these creatures are a nuisance, they are a menace only in winter, when they attack dormant crowns and consume the eyes that will make next year's shoots, and in mid spring, when they attack new growth. Fortunately there are excellent slug and snail repellents and killers available that will keep them under control. In early winter (November) when you cut down the dying foliage, cover the delphinium crowns with weathered boiler ashes or sharp sand for extra protection.

The delphinium is also reasonably disease-free. Rotting of the crowns sometimes occurs but this usually happens to plants that have been fed excessively to produce exhibition blooms. Late in the season delphiniums can be attacked by mildew, but as this usually happens when the flowering period is over, it can be ignored, there being little evidence that the plants suffer permanent damage. In some districts mildew appears quite early and when this happens, spray or dust with a sulphur-based compound.

Above: the greenhouse dianthus is particularly susceptible to red spider mite.

Dianthus (carnations and pinks) The most serious pest attacking greenhouse carnations is the red spider mite, a sure killer if it is not dealt with quickly. The sap-sucking debilitates the plants to such an extent that they become lifeless, brittle, strawy in appearance and eventually ruined. Other pests that attack carnations are thrips, caterpillars and greenfly. Greenfly are not just a nuisance but a menace. They suck the plants' sap and can transmit viruses from diseased plants to healthy ones. On outdoor pinks greenfly and thrips are sometimes troublesome in early summer (May). Young plants are attacked by the carnation fly.

Erica, *see* Calluna.

Euonymus Aphids and scale insects are the most common pests to attack euonymus. Leaf spot disease, indicated by brown spots on the leaves can cause serious disfigurement. Powdery mildew often affects *E. japonicus*. Euonymus are also liable to attack from honey fungus which can cause rapid death of the plant.

Ferns On the whole, ferns, both outside and under glass or in the home, are surprisingly free of pests and diseases. Leaf eelworm, tarsonemid mite, slugs, snails and caterpillars are the most likely troubles.

Flowering cherry, *see* Prunus.

Below: the principal enemies of the delphinium are slugs and snails.

Below: Euonymus alatus, *deciduous spindle, has several enemies.*

Far left: Fuchsia cordifolia, *a greenhouse species. Centre:* Gladiolus *Oscar (large-flowered). Above:* Iris *Golden Alps. Below:* Laburnum x vossii, *a profusely-flowering form.*

Fuchsia The plant can be severely damaged by capsid bugs. Whitefly can be found especially under glass, and should be controlled immediately it is seen. Fuchsias are seldom subject to disease though grey mould may damage the plants in winter if temperatures are too low and the soil and atmosphere too moist.

Geranium For the true hardy *Geranium* species and cultivars, see under Perennials. For the bedding and greenhouse geraniums, see *Pelargonium*.

Gladiolus Although about 20 pests and diseases attack gladioli, few are lethal. The most important ones to watch for and deal with promptly are dry rot, neck rot and scab, leaf spot or hard rot, thrips, aphids, slugs, snails and earwigs.

Hawthorn see *Crataegus*.

Heathers, see *Calluna*

Hebe (shrubby veronica) Hebe are little troubled by pests other than aphids, but they might be attacked by honey fungus or leaf-spot.

Hollyhock, see *Althaea*.

Hyacinths In wet seasons, hyacinths in the garden may suffer tulip fire (*Botrytis*), root rot and soft rot. In store, blue mould rot can be a nuisance especially if the bulbs are kept out of the ground beyond mid-October. As a rule, none of these diseases is serious.

Iris Ink disease can be serious on certain bulbous irises, particularly the winter flowering sorts. The tall and the dwarfer rhizomatous species and cultivars, particularly the many Bearded Hybrids are prone to attacks by slugs, snails, soft rhizome rot and leaf spot. Certain viruses can be locally troublesome.

Laburnum The only pests that attack laburnum seriously are leaf-cutter bees and leaf miners, both of which damage the leaves. The trees are, however, subject to attack by honey fungus, indicated by failure to flower properly, premature leaf fall and dieback of branches. If the infestation is serious, you must dig up the tree and burn it.

Lathyrus (sweet peas) Fortunately, there are relatively few pests and diseases that attack sweet peas and those that do can generally be treated or prevented fairly easily. When you are sowing seed, keep mice away with a light sprinkling of paraffin around the cold frame or stations. Slugs and snails can also be a danger. In early summer (May) caterpillars can damage the foliage and growing points. Greenfly start to become active in early or mid summer (May or June). It is, however, possible for aphids to transmit mosaic virus before a spray is effective, so it is wise to try to develop an eye for a diseased plant. Remove all such plants and burn them. Do not forget to wash clean the knife or scissors when you have finished. In some districts, birds of the tit family can puncture the young buds in search of pollen, and sparrows can also be a nuisance.

It must be emphasized – particularly if you grow sweet peas by the cordon method – that over-enrichment of the soil season after season, and over-stimulation by unnecessary nitrogenous fertilizers is best avoided, this being a common cause of plant disorders.

Lawns Various pests and diseases can be troublesome in the autumn.
EARTHWORMS While not themselves doing any damage to the grass, they make casts of fine, moist soil that are unsightly. If they are flattened by the mower they will cake hard and inhibit growth of grass. So brush off wormcasts before mowing. If you have a bad infestation and wish to eliminate the worms, apply either carbaryl or chlordane in the autumn according to the manufacturer's instructions.
LEATHERJACKETS These grubs of crane flies (or daddy longlegs) are active in autumn, eating the roots of grass and causing it to die out in patches.
FUSARIUM PATCH Probably one of the most common lawn diseases, it starts off as brown patches, that gradually increase in size and merge together. They are covered in white fungal threads. This disease is worse in poorly aerated turf – so spiking will help to prevent it.
CORTICUM DISEASE ('red thread') Seen as pinkish patches on the lawn with red fungus growths on them. Again the control is to apply a mercury-based fungicide, as above.
DOLLAR SPOT A less common fungus disease. It appears as small circles, about 5cm (2 in) in diameter, which are brown at first and later take on a bleached appearance. As soon as the trouble is noticed, treat with a mercury-based fungicide.
TOADSTOOLS These may appear on the lawn in autumn. If they are growing in a circle of dark green grass with a dead patch in the centre, then they are due to the fungus marasmius. The symptoms are popularly referred to as 'fairy rings'. This disease is difficult to control with chemicals, and the most effective treatment is to remove the turf and soil from the affected area and refill with fresh topsoil. Then re-turf or sow the area with grass seed.

Lilac, *see* Syringa.

Lilium Slug damage can be prevented by laying slug pellets round the plants. Lily beetle – another pest that causes serious damage – can be controlled with sprays of malathion. Leather jackets may attack the roots and bulbs.

Lily roots and basal plates are sometimes attacked by a fungus known as narcissus basal rot qv. Sometimes brown spots appear on the leaves – the result of attack by lily disease (*botrytis*).

Lilies are also subject to several virus diseases that can be avoided by buying guaranteed virus-free bulbs whenever possible, and digging up and burning any plants showing symptoms such as mottling of leaves and stunted growth.

Malus Malus is rather prone to attack from pests. Aphids, particularly the woolly variety, may attack the young leaves and fruits. The presence of these aphids is shown by the branches being covered with white, waxy, woolly tufts and the growth of galls.

Capsid bugs cause distortions by piercing the young leaf buds and fruit. Fruit tree red spider mites attack the undersides of the leaves, which turn bronze, wither and drop. The fruits of malus are sometimes holed by the larvae of the codling moth and apple sawfly.

Malus is liable to much the same diseases as the ordinary apple. These include apple mildew, which is shown by a white powdery layer on new growths and leaves.

Above: narcissi and daffodils are easy to grow and reasonably trouble free.

Apple scab produces brown or black scabs on the fruits.

Honey fungus could cause the rapid death of the tree unless it is brought under control in the early stages. An application of chemicals called Armillatox and Bray's Emulsion may possibly save the tree.

Maple, *see* Acer.

Mountain ash, *see* Sorbus.

Narcissus Although narcissi and daffodils are easy to grow and are seldom seriously decimated by pests and diseases, there are troubles which can be locally serious, especially where these bulbs are grown *en masse*. Eelworm, large and small narcissus flies are the primary pests. Among diseases, smoulder, leaf scorch, basal rot and viruses can be serious in some seasons.

Nerine Nerines are reasonably free from diseases, but heavy soil and excess moisture during the dormant period can produce bulb rot. Their only common complaint is a mild form of virus that produces streaking in the leaves, but this has no observable effect on flowering. More serious individual attacks, due to

Above: Paphiopedilum insigne, *a colourful 'slipper' orchid.*

Above: Pelargonium peltatum *should be protected from frosts.*

other viruses, are occasionally encountered. In such cases, the plant suffers loss of vigour. Mealy bug infestation occurs from time to time.

Orchids Orchids are less prone to pests and diseases than many other greenhouse plants. Ideal growing conditions are, in themselves, a deterrent to most greenhouse pests that thrive best in a hot, dry atmosphere.

Pests find their way into the greenhouse in two ways. The indigenous kinds enter from outside, attracted by the warmth of the greenhouse, but other pests are introduced on already-infested plants brought into the house.

RED SPIDER MITE This leaf-sucking mite is probably the most common pest found on orchids, mainly because it is extremely hard to detect until large colonies have built up and the damage caused to the undersides of the leaves can be clearly seen.

MEALY BUG This pest usually prefers the softer-leaved orchids and can be found mostly round the base of the plant and inside leaf bracts and folds – anywhere it can feel safe and dry. Damage only becomes noticeable where you have allowed large colonies to remain unchecked for some time. In this case the pest becomes apparent when yellow spots appear on the foliage.

SCALE INSECTS There are several different kinds of scale insect, all having in common a scaly membrane that covers them and provides protection.

OTHER PESTS Keep a constant watch for garden pests such as slugs, snails and aphids and take the usual precautions against them at once.

Leaf-sucking pests can also be the cause of introducing virus disease. Viruses can occur in any orchid, usually taking the form of white flecking on the foliage, that in turn becomes blackened as a secondary infection develops on the dead leaf cells. Although there is no known cure for virus disease, it can be arrested by improving the culture and general well-being of the plant. Various types of black spot and blemishes can occasionally be seen on the bulbs and foliage of orchids. Often these are nothing more than old foliage becoming marked with age prior to being naturally discarded by the plant. Watery marks on bulbs can occur where conditions are not completely suitable.

Prolonged cold combined with high humidity can cause various marks to appear. The answer is to increase warmth and ventilation. Bulbs damaged in this way are best treated by rubbing sulphur into the blister to try and dry it up and to prevent spreading.

Pansy, see *Viola*.

Pelargonium (pot, zonal, regal geraniums) During the past 20 years rust disease of zonal pelargoniums has spread rapidly throughout the world. It can be locally serious and should be watched for. Viruses also should be looked for at the height of the growing season. Blackleg is often troublesome when cuttings have been in their propagating pots for a week or so. Aphids come and go, and under glass whitefly can be serious.

Perennials All the popular herbaceous and evergreen perennials are remarkably trouble-free plants but they are not without pest and disease troubles. Among pests, aphids, capsid bugs, caterpillars (including cutworms), froghoppers, slugs and snails are all likely to occur from time to time but rarely seriously. Viruses and mildew turn up now and then as does leaf spot and crown gall. The last mentioned is most likely to be on chrysanthemum, hollyhock, lupin and phlox.

Pinks see *Dianthus*.

Primula Pot primulas in the greenhouse or home can suffer from aphids, red spider mite and whitefly. Primrose, poly-

Above: Primula malacoides. *Above right: the stems, leaves and berries of the pyracantha are all vulnerable. Below right: the hardy rhododendron hybrid* Gomer Waterer. *Far right: certain roses are almost disease-free.*

anthus and others are sometimes attacked by slugs, birds, bryobia mites, aphids and mildew.

Prunus Birds, and bullfinches in particular, eat the flowering buds in winter. Aphids, cherry blackfly and caterpillars can infest the leaves.

Flowering cherries can be attacked by silver leaf – this is a fungus that causes the leaves to turn a silvery colour. You can minimize the risk by not cutting any wood away during winter – this should be done in the summer, when the wound is likely to heal quickly.

Pyracantha Stems and leaves are sometimes affected by aphids, particularly woolly aphids, that are detected by the presence of white, waxy tufts; spray with derris or malathion to control them. Scale insects are another menace. They make the plant sticky, and sooty moulds develop. Spray with diazonin or malathion if the infestation is heavy.

As with other species belonging to the ROSACEAE family, pyracantha are likely to be attacked by fireblight. A disease peculiar to pyracantha is pyracantha scab, indicated by an olive-brown or black coating on the leaves and berries.

Rhododendron Given the acid soil they need, and adequate moisture, rhododendrons are seldom seriously attacked by pests and diseases. In some areas bud blast can greatly reduce the flowering potential of a bush, and vine weevil makes the leaves unsightly. Rhododendron bug, whitefly and honey fungus can, in certain areas be a serious problem Where there is a bit too much lime, iron deficiency will show up in the leaves and the plant will lack vigour. See also under Azalea.

Rosa (Rose) There are a number of roses that, under most garden conditions, can be said to be reasonably or almost completely free from disease. The hybrid tea roses in this category include: Pink Favorite and Honey Favorite (both outstanding), Peace, Grandpa Dickson, Wendy Cussons, Rose Gaujard, Ernest H. Morse, Red Devil, Fragrant Cloud, Chicago Peace and Gail Borden.

Some healthy floribundas are: Southampton, Matangi, Sarabande, Escapade, Chinatown and Evelyn Fison, and among the climbers are Aloha, Mermaid and Golden Showers.

The rugosas, Chinas and a number of the species are outstanding among the shrub roses, but many of the others are so tough that they can shrug off attacks by mildew and black spot without coming to any harm, though this will not prevent them looking rather unsightly in late summer if they remain unsprayed.

Quite a large number of other roses could be added to the list given above, based on individual growers' experience in particular gardens or in particular districts. Even moving a variety as prone to mildew as Rosemary Rose from one part of a single garden to another has been known to bring about a cure. Dryness about the roots and lack of proper air circulation often encourages mildew, and the purer the air the more black spot flourishes. In industrial areas, where there is sulphur in the atmosphere from factory chimneys, black spot will be no problem, and it is ironic that the creation of smokeless zones, so beneficial to most things, has caused this rose

ROSES – a guide to fungicides and insecticides

FUNGICIDES FOR OUTDOOR ROSES

Active ingredient	Proprietary name	Powdery mildew	Black spot	Rust
maneb	Maneb WP		★★	★★
zineb	Dithane		★★	★★
thiram	ICI Garden Fungicide		★★	★★
captan	Orthocide or Captan		★★	
dinocap	Karathane or Dinocap	★★		
folpet	Murphy Rose Fungicide	★	★★	★
benomyl	Benlate	★★★	★★	
triforine	Gesal Rose Mildew Treatment	★★★	★★	□
oxycarboxin	ICI Plantvax 75			★★★
thiophanate-methyl	Mildothane	★★	★★	
mancozeb	Dithane		★★	★★

Home greenhouse insecticides

For all pests except mites, either: resmethrin + pyrethrum (Sprayday), or bioresmethrin (Copper Garden Spray). Against red spider mites, only water or white oil (eg Volck) are recommended. The following have systemic action: formothion, dimethoate, menazon and fenitrothion (eg Fentro, Accothion). Trichlorphon (Dipterex), while not systemic, can penetrate the leaf-blade.

Compatability guide

Any two wettable powder (WP) fungicides can be mixed with one liquid insecticide, or two if one is Dipterex 80 (a solution).

More than two liquid pesticides should not be mixed together unless a trial has shown them to be compatible. For this generalization ICI Garden Fungicide (a colloidal liquid) can be considered a WP. When three or more pesticides are to be sprayed together they should be diluted separately and mixed together immediately before spray application.

INSECTICIDES FOR OUTDOOR ROSES

Insecticide	Aphids	Thrips	Capsids	Leaf hopper	Scale Insects	Caterpillars	Leaf-rolling sawfly	Chafers	Leaf miners
formothion dimethoate	★★★			★★★	★				
malathion diazinon	★★	★	★	★★	★★	★			
menazon	★★★			□					
gamma-BHC	★	★	★★	★		★		★	★★
trichlorphon						★★★	★★		★★
fenitrothion	★★	★	★	★★	□	★★	★★	★	★□

★★★ very active ★★ moderately active ★ slightly active □ more evidence required WP wettable powder

disease to spread into areas where it was not known before.

So the experience of a grower of a particular variety in one part of the country may be very different from one elsewhere, but the roses named above have been found to be some of the best in all conditions.

Not everyone, however, will want to grow just these varieties, and if you have an established garden, you will have to deal with the roses already growing there, that may not be so disease resistant.

Chemical fungicide sprays are expensive, and spraying itself is not the most enjoyable of occupations. Many people feel, too, that it is risky to use chemicals, about whose long-term effects we really know very little. One has only to think back to the time, not so long ago, when DDT was used on a world-wide scale against insect pests and then was suddenly found to be harmful and withdrawn from sale, to see the force of this argument. All of which adds up to not spraying more than you have to.

If there is no sign of black spot in your garden, do not spray against it; or wait until you see the first signs of mildew before you take action. In some years it will be much less prevalent than others and only touch one or two roses.

However, there are areas, and the

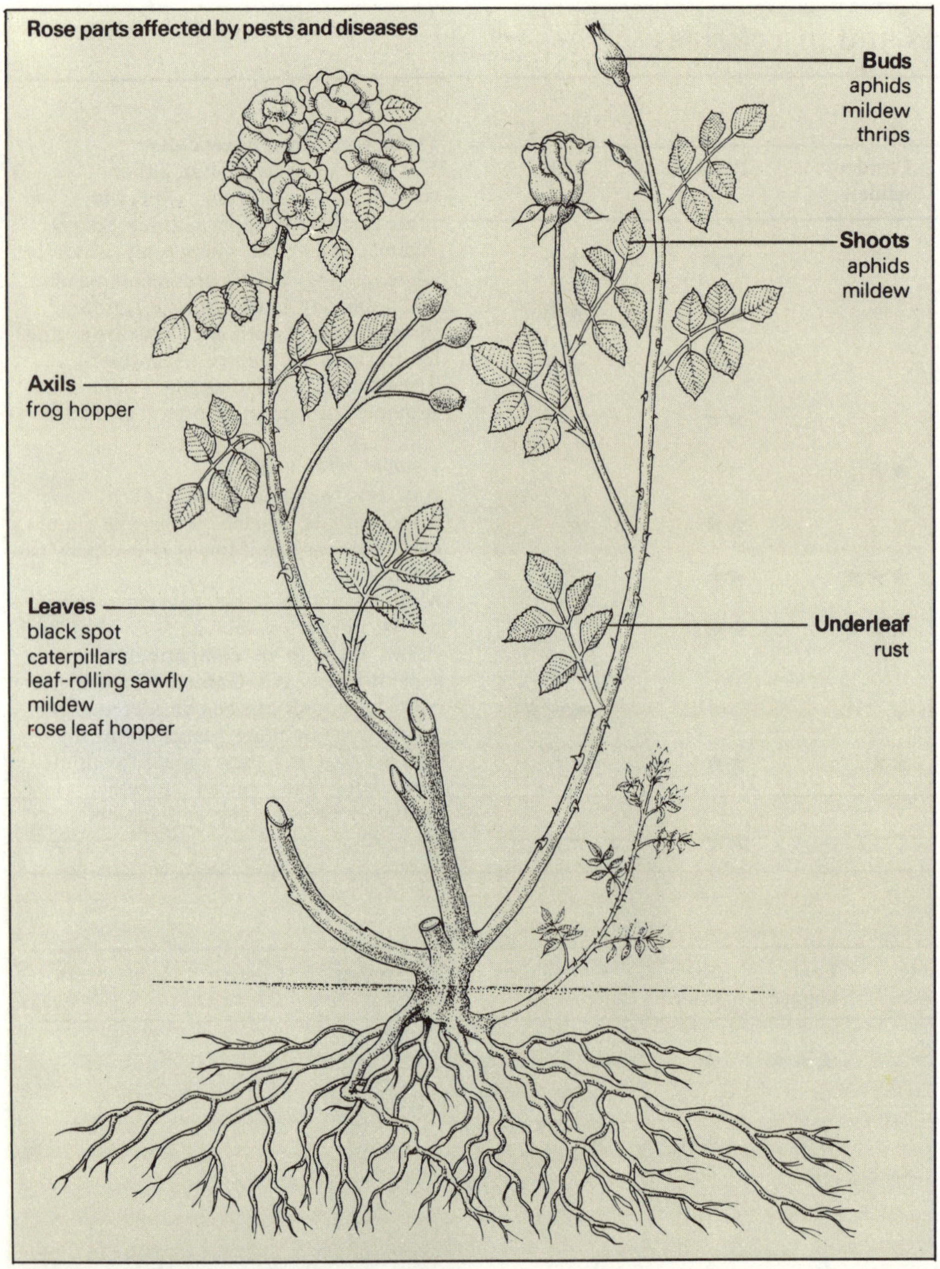

Left: herbicide is easier to apply to roses with a sprinkle bar attachment.
Below: blackspot, which appears on rose leaves only in clean-air districts, is carried by airborne spores and usually becomes apparent around the middle of the summer.

south-west of England is one, where black spot is always a serious problem, and there it is usual to have to carry out preventative spraying each year before the disease appears, and probably to top up regularly, as often as every ten days or so, for the rest of the summer. In other places, rust is the trouble, but find out from local growers what diseases your roses are likely to get, and judge from your own experience before acting.

HOW AND WHEN TO SPRAY

Wherever you live, you are unlikely not to have to spray against anything at all, be it insects or disease spores, so a few general points about spraying should be born in mind. It is best to use a spray that produces a fine mist. Do not spray in hot sunshine, or the leaves of the rose may scorch – evening is the best time; spray sufficiently to wet the plants all over, but not to the extent of leaving them dripping, which is an awful waste of expensive liquid. Do spray the undersides of the leaves as well as the upper surfaces.

SYSTEMIC SPRAYS These penetrate into the tissue of the plant. In some cases they will circulate with the sap, but not all sprays do this equally well, which is why it is important to wet the whole rose. Systemics have the great advantage, of course, that they are not washed off by rain and so will remain effective for several weeks.

PESTICIDES AND FUNGICIDES

Great strides have been made in recent years with pesticides and fungicides. Greenfly infestation should not be a serious problem any more; mildew is largely under control; an oxycarboxin spray such as Plantvax 75 is a certain treatment for rust; and black spot, while not mastered, can at least be controlled to a large extent in all but the worst areas.

Our chart, based on one prepared by the Royal National Rose Society, should prove a useful guide as to the best sprays to be used for the different diseases and insects. As indicated, many of these chemicals can be mixed together, so that you can spray against everything (if you are unlucky enough to suffer from everything) at one and the same time. The warning given in the Note below should, however, be stressed. Make quite sure that your particular sprays are compatible. Otherwise you run the risk of losing all the leaves from your roses or of causing scorch.

Above: Rose leaves attacked by rust. Fortunately this disease is not as widespread as either mildew or black spot, nor are all varieties liable to attack, as a serious invasion can kill.
Left: rose aphids (Macrosiphum rosae) *however, attack* all *roses, wild and cultivated, and can be extremely destructive. At about 5mm ($\frac{1}{5}$ in) long these are among the largest of the species of aphid. There can be much variation in the colour of aphids, although pink and green predominate.*

MILDEW
This is the most prevalent of the rose diseases, and is carried by airborne spores from one plant to another. The first signs are generally small, grey, powdery-looking patches on the leaves and on the flower-stalks and undersides of the buds. In bad cases, the mildew will spread over the entire plant, distorting growth and preventing the second crop of flowers from opening properly. Mildew will not kill a rose, but it will ruin its appearance.

If treated promptly, mildew can nowadays be controlled, but the spraying of vigorous climbers can be a problem if they are high up on the wall of a house. Ramblers, which as a class are subject to mildew, should preferably never be planted against house walls where air circulation will be poor.

BLACK SPOT
This is also carried by airborne spores, and usually appears first around the middle of the summer on the older, lower leaves of rose bushes. The small, circular black spots rapidly grow in size, the rest of the leaf yellows, and eventually dies and drops off. Bad attacks can completely defoliate a rose and this lack of leaves, apart from being unsightly, weakens the plant and can kill it over several seasons of repeated attacks. Spraying will help control, but no real cure has been found. Ideally, affected leaves should be picked off and burned to prevent the black spot spores from spreading.

Spores of both black spot and mildew can overwinter on leaves left on the ground, and also on the rose stems and stumps that have not been properly pruned back. Winter spraying against the trouble with Bordeaux mixture should be done at least once, and preferably twice.

RUST
Fortunately, this is not as widespread as mildew or black spot, and only certain varieties are usually liable to attack, for a serious invasion of your garden by rust can kill the roses. Until quite recently it was recommended that badly-affected plants should be dug up and burned, but now a spray of oxycarboxin gives complete control. Rust can be recognized by the formation of orange pustules on the undersides of the leaves, and it should be dealt with without delay.

These, then, are the rose diseases that most rose growers will have to deal with at some time. There are also insect pests, against which modern insecticides give very good protection, but as with diseases, you also need to be able to recognize the insect enemies to be able to deal with them. The following are the most common and troublesome.

APHIDS OR GREENFLY
Probably too well known to need description except to say that those which infest the young shoots and buds of roses can be brown and pink as well as green. They suck the sap of the plant and exude a sticky substance known as honeydew, on which a sooty mould forms. Increase is incredibly rapid, so spray promptly.

THRIPS
Small, black insects that move with great speed over the plant and drop off if disturbed, only to climb back later. Hot, dry summers seem to suit thrips; nibbled-looking buds are likely to be their work, and distorted flowers the outcome. Some varieties of rose are, for some reason, much more prone to attack than others, notably Ophelia and its descendants, Mme Butterfly and Lady Sylvia. One cure for thrips is said to be the covering of the beds under the roses with metal foil, as the thrips do not appear to like the reflected light coming from below! Hardly the ideal solution for most gardens.

FROG HOPPER OR CUCKOO SPIT
Small, green insects that hide themselves in a blob of white froth, usually at a joint between a stem or leaf and a side shoot. The nymph sucks the sap of the rose. Either the fingers (if the attack is limited), or a jet of water, should be used to remove the froth before spraying.

ROSE LEAF HOPPER
Very small, pale yellow insects, that leap high in the air if disturbed. They cause mottling of the rose leaves, and the presence of their cast-off white skins on the undersides of the leaves is a sure sign that leaf hoppers are about.

CATERPILLARS
In a mild attack, these can be removed by hand but Dipterex is a most effective spray. It will penetrate the leaf, and so will deal with caterpillars that have doubled a leaf round themselves, as some do when they are feeding on it.

LEAF-ROLLING SAWFLY
This pest appears to be on the increase. The name is very descriptive, for the sawfly lays its eggs on the leaves that then curl up lengthwise, protecting the grub feeding within. This makes it difficult to reach with sprays, which are only really effective if applied before an attack, which in itself is difficult to predict. Otherwise, tedious though it may be, removal of the rolled-up leaves is recommended to prevent the larvae moving on to another leaf when they have had enough of the first one.

NOTE Capsids, scale insects, chafer grubs and leaf miners can also be a problem on roses and should be controlled with the appropriate insecticide. Most fungicides active against black spot will also control downy mildew.

Mixtures of several pesticides are not recommended because experience has shown that while some may give good results, straight insecticides are better value and less liable to cause scorch.

Seedlings The failure of seeds to germinate is not always the fault of the seed. Pests and diseases may take their toll, especially in spring when we tend to sow seeds before the soil is warm enough to induce germination. Seeds that lie in a cold, wet soil may rot. Mice have a passion for pea and broad bean seeds, and can decimate a sowing. How they find the seeds is a mystery. If their presence is suspected, a mouse-trap or two will soon account for them, but make sure that domestic pets cannot get at them. Birds can be a nuisance where grass seed has been sown, but nowadays most grass seed offered for sale is treated with a bird-repellent; this makes the seed unpalatable without doing the birds any harm.

Some diseases are seed-borne. Notable examples in the vegetable world are celery leaf-spot and lettuce mosaic virus and, in the flower zone, seedling-blight of zinnias. To protect the seeds from these and other pests and diseases, a seed dressing can be used. These dressings are usually based on HCH (BHC) and captan, and can be obtained from any gardening centre or hardware store. Use them strictly according to the makers' instructions. There is no need to dress celery seed; in nearly every case, this is done before it is sent out. Because of this, surplus celery or celeriac seed should never be used for medicinal purposes. The small size and soft nature of seedlings make them more vulnerable to certain pests and diseases. In particular, damping disease should be looked for especially where the seedlings have come up very thickly. Flea beetles, slugs, snails, cutworms, leather jackets (cranefly grubs), wireworms and woodlice can all be nuisance from time to time.

Sorbus Apple canker produces severe cankers on the bark of sorbus and sometimes kills large shoots. Fireblight, which blackens and shrivels the blooms and gradually kills the branches that carry brown and withered leaves, is likely to attack the sorbus, so cut it out and burn the infected wood. Honey fungus may also attack a sorbus and destroy it quickly.

Caterpillars can be a nuisance in late spring and early summer (April-May) and birds eat the berries. Where the alternate host, juniper occurs, mountain ash rust may be present.

Above left: seedling blight is a fungus infection. Above: Syringa *(lilac).*

Sweet pea, see *Lathyrus*.

Syringa (Lilac) Leaves are sometimes tunnelled by lilac leaf miners. Flowers are sometimes killed by late frost, which also causes young shoots to die back. Such affected tissue are liable to become covered with a greyish-brown fungus due to grey mould (*botrytis*). Honey fungus is also liable to attack and kill syringa. Brown spots on leaves and blackened, withered shoots are due to lilac blight; treat by cutting affected branches back to healthy tissue. A spray of Bordeaux Mixture, repeated if necessary, can also help. Silver leaf is another disease that might attack syringa.

Trees and Shrubs Ornamental trees and shrubs are subject to attack by large numbers of pests and diseases, but fortunately many of these troubles have no major ill effects on appearance or growth. However, some infestations can be very damaging, so the wise gardener keeps a close watch on the health of his plants and is prepared to take immediate action as and when necessary. Here we identify the more important pests and diseases, and advise on how to deal with them. Problems relating to specific trees and shrubs, such as roses, are dealt with individually in alphabetical order.

PESTS

Prominent among pests of ornamental trees and shrubs are aphids.

APHIDS Blackfly and greenfly are all-too-common garden pests, so it is important to keep a sharp look-out for early signs of attack and to take remedial action before the infestation builds up to damaging levels. In particular, ornamental prunus species need to be checked over at bud burst since leaf-curling aphids frequently appear at this stage. Lonicera (honeysuckle) and viburnum species also need special attention because of the large number of blackfly attacks.

Greenfly and blackfly are generally easy to control but the beech aphid, and the woolly aphid that attacks malus (flowering crab), cotoneaster, pyracantha (firethorn) and chaenomeles (flowering quince), are more resistant because of their protective covering of white, woolly wax. This necessitates the use of strong, forceful sprays such as malathion or formothion to aid penetration.

SCALE INSECTS These can be very harmful because they not only reduce the vigour of the host plant but they also stunt young growth and cause yellowing of the foliage. Like aphids, they feed by sucking the plant sap and produce honeydew that in later development assumes the appearance of disfiguring

Below: mussel scale insects feeding on an apple.

Above: scale insects firmly attached to the underside of a bay leaf.

sooty moulds. Unlike the majority of insects, however, they spend much of their life in one place firmly attached to the plant surface. Because of their scaly covering, most species look like miniature limpets or mussels, but they are difficult to spot because of their lack of movement and their natural coloration.

Brown scale, mussel scale, nut scale, willow scale and horse chestnut scale attack a wide range of broad-leaved plants, while juniper scale, on the other hand, has a number of conifer hosts such as cypress, juniper and thuya (arborvitae). Beech and yew scale, however, are restricted to their named hosts – the former, incidentally, is more easily spotted than are most scales, being covered with a white mass of woolly wax. Similar wax also envelops the eggs of the horse chestnut scale when these are produced between early and mid summer (late May and early June).

Because of the protection given by their scaly covering, these pests are not easy to control. Repeat sprays with diazinon, malathion or pirimiphosmethyl, starting in early or mid summer (late May or early June) can be effective. Nevertheless, it is still good policy to scrape off the larger scales gently before applying the spray, as these are least likely to be affected.

RED SPIDER MITE These mites are extremely small, being only just visible to the naked eye. They, too, feed by sucking plant sap, and as well as reducing plant vigour they also cause the infected leaves to become speckled and ultimately completely yellowed, silvered or bronzed.

Bryobia and fruit tree mites can, and do, attack many broad-leaved trees and shrubs. However, conifers such as cedar, cypress, juniper and thuya, and some species of pine, are subject to invasion by the conifer spinning mite.

Spraying against mites is best done in warm, sunny weather when these pests are active. It must, however, be emphasized that repeat treatments may be needed to obtain good control. Furthermore, not all insecticides are active against mites, so it is advisable to select a product that contains at least one – or more – of the following chemicals: dicofil, dimethoate, formothion, malathion or pirimiphosmethyl.

CATERPILLARS These larval forms of butterflies and moths can be very damaging to the foliage of many shrubs and trees. Fortunately, most types are readily controlled by general garden insecticides such as derris.

Leaf-tying species and those that cause the leaves to roll up present special problems, however. Against these, it is necessary to use systemic or partially-systemic chemicals that can penetrate the leaf tissue. It is even more difficult to deal with those species that protect themselves by spinning a cover of webbing over their colony. In this situation, if the webbing has been completed before the pests are detected, it is better to prune off the infected shoots before spraying the rest of the foliage.

LEAF MINERS Leaf 'mines' are produced by the grubs of small moths and flies. They show up as either white, convoluted, linear tracks on the leaves, or roundish blisters. They can be found on syringa (lilac), ligustrum (privet), lonicera and azalea, but are most common on ilex (holly).

Below: weevil grubs feed on roots, bulbs, and corms, and on the foliage of shrubs.

At the first sign of infection, which is usually in early summer (May), give a thorough spraying with a general insecticide, and follow this up with two or three repeat applications. These treatments will deal with developing eggs, but for the control of grubs within the leaf tissue it is necessary to use a systemic or partially-systemic chemical like diazinon.

WEEVILS The grubs of these small insects feed on roots, bulbs and corms, but the principal damage to shrubs is caused by the adults feeding on the foliage. The vine weevil, that also attacks a wide range of other shrubs, cuts characteristic notches in the leaf margin, while leaf weevils make holes in the leaves. The latter species may also feed on blossom petals.

Attacks by clay-coloured weevils are indicated not only by the presence of holes and notches in the leaves, but also by damage to the bark of the shoots. These weevils may additionally gnaw through the petioles of leaves and the pedicels of flowers, and can sometimes destroy buds.

Some degree of control can be achieved by foliar sprays, but these should be reinforced by spraying or dusting the ground around the infested plants.

DISEASES

One of the most lethal diseases is the honey (or bootlace) fungus, that kills many varieties of ornamental and fruit-bearing trees and shrubs.

HONEY FUNGUS This spreads by runner-like strands that grow along the roots and finally up the trunk inside the bark. The first sign of attack is the dying back of some branches, which is then followed by the death of the whole shrub or tree. If the upper roots or the base of the trunk are stripped of bark, the fungus threads can be seen, resembling either white lace or black bootlaces.

No really reliable control measures are currently available, so infected bushes should be dug up and as much as possible of the root system removed and then burned. Disinfect the soil around the bush with 2 per cent formaldehyde (250ml/9 fl oz of 38 per cent formalin to 12 litres/3 gal water) before replanting with shrubs or trees.

FIRE BLIGHT In the UK this very destructive disease of pears and apples must be reported to your Local Authority. It also attacks pyracantha, crataegus (hawthorn or may), stranvaesia, and both whitebeam and mountain ash sorbus. Initially, the tip of the infected shoot wilts, and drops of bacterial ooze can be seen on the infected stem. Later the leaves and stem become brown. Cut out and burn the infected branches immediately, and paint the cut surfaces with a white lead paint.

Even if you merely suspect the presence of the disease, you should still notify your Local Authority, so that they can advise on exactly what action to take.

WILT DISEASE Wilt is a major disease of clematis and results in one or more shoots dying back very rapidly, usually to ground level. Mature plants may later throw up new shoots but the disease could be fatal to newly-planted clematis.

Some protection can be given to established and developing shoots by spraying with copper fungicide. It is, however, better to plant the clematis rather deeply to ensure that there are some dormant buds below soil level. It is also good insurance to layer one or more shoots, thus establishing multiple plants.

Syringa (lilac) and some other ornamentals are liable to attack by verticillium wilt. This soil-borne disease starts at the root and then moves up the conducting tissue into the trunk, causing wilting and browning of the leaves and stems. Remove and burn infected plants, and disinfect the soil with formalin solution before replanting.

CANKERS These are caused by bacteria or fungi that attack the shoots and cause the development of sunken patches in the bark. They commonly girdle smaller branches and shoots, leading to the death of all growth above the canker. On larger branches the cankers are usually restricted to one side.

Prune back all badly-infected small shoots to clean, healthy wood, and pare away and destroy cankered patches on larger branches. Afterwards, seal the cuts with canker paint. In the case of the very damaging bacterial canker of flowering cherries, some protection can be obtained by giving three sprays with a copper fungicide, starting in early autumn (end of August), and repeating the dose at three-week intervals.

Willows suffer from lesions produced by anthracnose fungus. In this case, repeated sprays with a copper fungicide in early summer (May) are recommended.

POWDERY MILDEW This shows up as whitish, powdery patches on the leaves, and is particularly troublesome on euonymus (spindle), mahonia, clematis, hydrangea and crataegus.

Initiate repeat treatments with dinocap, benomyl or thiram at the first sign of attack and continue until the disease is under control.

LEAF SPOTS A wide variety of shrubs are attacked by this type of disease. Control can usually be obtained by giving a series of sprays with benomyl, captan or thiram at 10–14 day intervals.

ROOT DEATH Reliable nurserymen would never offer diseased plants. But there is one serious disease of shrubs whose symptoms you should be able to recognize. Conifers and heathers are prone to attack by a fungus called phytophthora that causes the roots to rot and the plants to die. It affects some other shrubs too, such as rhododendrons,

Below left: fruiting bodies of the honey fungus, Armillaria mellea. *Below: the leaves of a pear tree which has been attacked by fire blight.*

Above: a healthy specimen of Viburnum sargentii. *Above right: the modestly-coloured* Viola odorata *noted for its particularly sweet scent.*

and is highly infectious – it can spread like wildfire in a nursery. Obviously you do not want to introduce it into your garden. Conifers suffering from this disease lose their natural foliage and turn greyish. They start to die from the base upwards. Heathers have similar symptoms and also the tips of the shoots wilt in the early stages of infection. Rhododendrons generally show a somewhat stunted appearance, the leaves being smaller than normal and often of a pale colour.

Tulipa Although a spring display of tulips is rarely ruined, there are several potentially serious diseases which are likely to strike during wet springs. Tulip fire is the worst, with grey bulb rot as a runner up. Blue mould rot often attacks bulbs being stored especially if they are not planted until November or December. Mice and slugs can also be minor pests of bulbs before they begin to grow above ground.

Viburnum Leaf-curling aphids and whiteflies sometimes infest viburnum. The presence of whitefly is indicated by the undersides of the leaves being covered with black scales fringed with white wax. *V. tinus* is particularly prone to attack from these pests.

Grey mould disease can also be troublesome on viburnum.

Viola (pansy and violet) These plants are little troubled with pests. Irregular spots with a thin brown margin, or yellow with a dark green centre that often falls out, giving a shot-hole effect, indicates leaf spot. Pansy sickness is indicated when the leaves turn yellow and the plants wilt, and the stem bases and underground parts rot. Do not put new plants in the same positions because the sickness is soil-borne. Yellow to orange or brown pustules on swollen, distorted stems show the presence of rust. Cucumber mosaic virus is indicated by curling, yellow-mottled leaves and stunted flowers showing white streaks. In some years, either powdery or downy mildew can be troublesome. Aphids are always a likely pest though seldom serious. Sweet violets usually get attacked by the violet leaf midge.

Water plants Most of the troubles which inflict the foliage and flowers of water plants are the same as those for perennials (qv). Some submerged aquatics are destroyed by pond snails. eg golden club (*Orontium*) and water soldier (Stratiotes). The great pond snail (*Limnaea stagnalis*) is the worst offender. Water lilies have their own special aphid and beetle pests. Both live on the surface of the floating leaves and are best dealt with by frequently hosing them off into the water where they drown or are eaten by fish.

Whitbeam, see *Sorbus*.

A-Z FRUIT AND VEGETABLES ATTACKED

Almond Peach leaf curl is the only disease of any importance and this can be severe.

Apples Pest and disease control is very important in growing a good crop of apples. At first this might seem to be a daunting task because there are nearly 50 pests and diseases that can attack apples alone. Fortunately however, only a relatively small number are sufficiently common to pose a serious threat.

These are: aphids, apple capsid, apple sawfly, apple sucker, codlin moth, spider mite (fruit tree), tortrix moth caterpillars, winter moth, apple scab, mildew (powdery) and canker.

APPLE PESTS

The following pests are the ones you are most likely to find in your garden. There are two types – those that spend their entire lifecycle on the tree, and those that infest the leaves, fruit and bark in one or other of the stages of their lifecycle.

APHIDS The various types of greenfly that attack apples overwinter as eggs on the bark of the trees. These eggs hatch out at about the same time the fruit buds begin to open, and the emerging greenfly then infest the young leaves and shoots.

APPLE CAPSID These pests also overwinter as eggs on the bark of the tree, and hatching again starts about the time that the young flower-buds are opening. The young bugs puncture the leaves, shoots and fruits, causing distortion and red spotting of the leaves, and producing rough, russet-coloured pits and pimples on the fruit.

APPLE SAWFLY Adult sawfly lay their eggs singly in slits that they cut in the base of the flower. The egg hatches out shortly after petal-fall (when most of the petals have been shed), and the young larva bores a hole into the apple core. It then moves on to a second fruitlet and repeats the operation. Finally, when it is mature, it falls to the ground where it spins its cocoon.

Above: codling moth larva in apple.
Below left and right: external and internal damage to an apple by capsid larvae.
Opposite: a healthy vegetable garden.

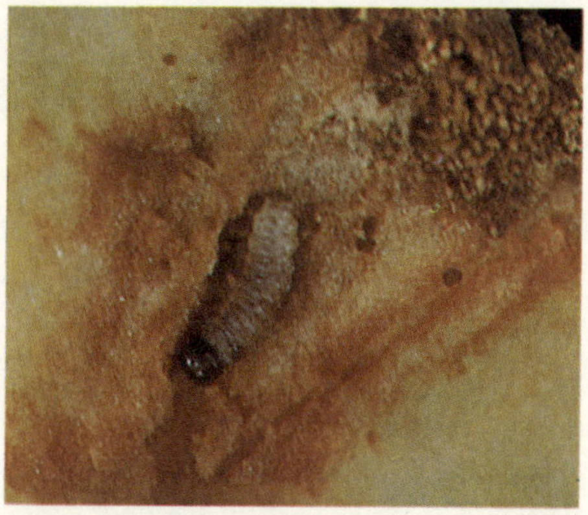

APPLE SUCKER Yet another pest that spends the winter in the egg stage on the bark. Hatching occurs during blossom-time and the suckers then feed on the leaves and flowers, often causing the blossom-trusses to turn brown, as if killed by frost.

CODLING MOTH These moths can emerge over a fairly long period from early summer to early autumn (May to early August), but the main hatching period is from mid to late summer (late June to mid July). They lay their eggs on the leaves and fruit, and the emerging

Left: winter moth caterpillars feeding on young apple leaves. Above: canker on the trunk of a pear tree. Right: healthy apple buds and buds affected with powdery mildew.

caterpillars then eat their way into the centre of the apples, leaving only a small entry hole. The mature caterpillars finally leave the fruit and spin their cocoons under loose bark or in other sheltered spots. When the ripe fruit is cut open, the core and exit passage can be seen to be full of frass (refuse left by the larva).

FRUIT TREE RED SPIDER MITE This pest winters as bright red, spherical eggs on the tree bark. Hatching begins at the pink-bud stage (when the buds show pink), and is complete within 3–4 weeks. The mites feed on the undersides of the leaves, causing speckling and bronzing of the foliage; severe outbreaks can kill the tree.

TORTRIX MOTH CATERPILLARS At least three species of tortrix are harmful to apples; one species causes damage both in the early flowering stage and again towards late summer (late June to early July), but the others restrict their attacks to mid summer (June). All three types cause serious damage to the skin of the apples.

WINTER MOTH Eggs of this pest laid on the bark during winter hatch out as the flower-buds are opening. The caterpillars feed on the young foliage and then fall to the ground where they pupate in the soil.

WOOLLY APHID This aphid passes the whole of its lifecycle on the tree, although it is not readily visible in winter. When it becomes active in mid or late spring (March or April), it secretes a white, wool-like substance that makes the closely-packed colonies very obvious. They puncture the bark whilst feeding, which results in the development of a lumpy, callus growth on the infected branches and twigs.

CONTROL OF APPLE PESTS

In following any programme of spraying to control pests, always remember to stop all such treatment as soon as the blossoms begin to open, otherwise the spray will kill the bees that will just have started pollination.

WINTER WASHES Since most of the major apple pests pass the winter in egg form on the bark of the trees, one approach to their control is to use winter washes of insecticides. These can either be tar oil or DNOC/petroleum products. Both these types of spray need to be applied at very high volume so as literally to wash the trees. Both are rather obnoxious to use, and protective clothing should be worn. Furthermore they are damaging to grass and other green plants and so are not easy to use with safety in garden conditions.

SPRING AND SUMMER SPRAYS These were originally used merely as supplements to the winter washes. With the ready availability of modern, very effective insecticides, however, they can now be used as complete replacements for the winter treatments. A programme of sprays, based on a good general insecticide such as dimethoate, fenitrothion or malathion, gives effective pest control with the minimum of effort. See the accompanying chart for a programme of six sprays.

WOOLLY APHIDS These require special treatment if an infestation occurs. They should be given drenching sprays with dimethoate, malathion or menazon. Repeat treatments may be necessary to deal with any survivors. The best time to apply the spray is between petal-fall and mid summer (June).

APPLE DISEASES

Apart from the diseases that attack the leaves, bark and fruit, there are also those that occur during storage; these are not dealt with here.

APPLE SCAB This shows up first as velvety, olive-green patches on the leaves. Early infection of the young fruitlets can later develop into ugly, dark brown calluses on the mature fruit, whilst heavy infection of the leaves causes premature leaf drop. The disease can develop at any time, from the early growth stages through to harvest. In practice, however, the early infections are the most important, since effective control measures at this time greatly reduce the build-up of the disease.

APPLE POWDERY MILDEW This disease carries over from one season to the next in infected buds. The primary infectors are easily recognized at bud-burst since the emerging growth is completely white and powdery. Subsequent spread of the disease is greatly reduced if all such growth is cut off and burnt at an early stage in its development.

CANKER This disease affects the wood of the tree, cankers first showing up as sunken areas on the bark. These can then spread completely round smaller shoots, causing them to die. On larger branches the damage is more usually restricted to one side only.

CONTROL OF APPLE DISEASES

Effective control of apple scab and

Left: bean with blackfly infestation.
Above: cabbage white butterfly.

powdery mildew can be obtained by spraying with suitable fungicides when the disease is first noticed. Benomyl, captan and thiram and various sulphur products all give good control of scab. All of these, with the exception of captan, are also active against mildew. When captan is used against scab, therefore, add dinocap to control the mildew.

Cankers that have not yet girdled the branch can be dealt with by cutting out the diseased tissue and then protecting the cut with a pruning paint. When the branch is completely encircled by the canker, the only remedy is to cut it back to clean, healthy wood. Here again, the cut surface needs to be painted for protection against fresh infections.

Apricot The most common enemies of apricots are caterpillars, silver leaf disease and a condition known as dieback.

Artichoke Globe artichokes are generally pest and disease free, but slugs may attack the young growth in the spring, so sprinkle slug pellets around the base of the plants. Jerusalem artichokes are remarkably pest free. Take care, however, that slugs do not get at stored tubers.

Asparagus Asparagus is prone to one or two pests and diseases. Good hygiene, in particular the cutting and burning of old, yellowed ferns, is one of the best preventive methods. see Asparagus beetle, Asparagus fly and Asparagus rust.

Aubergine These are usually free from pests and diseases, the red spider mite being a possible exception.

Beans Broad beans suffer severely from attacks of black fly. Chocolate spot can also be troublesome where rainfall is high.
French beans are troubled by black fly and slugs can be a problem too. Runner beans suffer from few problems apart from drought, but growing plants can be affected by black fly.

Beans, Broad Chocolate spot is the commonest disease of this crop. It shows up as chocolate-coloured spots on the leaves and pods and as dark stripes on the stems. At the first sign of attack the plants should be sprayed with copper fungicide and then repeat sprays given at intervals of 14 days. Broad beans are most susceptible to attack when grown in waterlogged conditions, so getting the soil into good condition before sowing the seed reduces the risk of infection. Broad beans also suffer severely from attacks of black fly.

Beans, Runner and French Root and foot rots can be troublesome. So the use of seed dressings, coupled with crop rotation, is to be recommended.

Beetroot Blackfly and boron deficiency can be a problem when growing beetroot. In certain seasons and areas, mosaic and beet yellows viruses can be troublesome.

Blackberry Raspberry beetle grubs and blackberry mites can spoil the fruits, and capsid bugs and aphids attack shoots and young leaves. On occasions, powdery mildew, rust, crown gall and virus may occur.

Blackcurrant *see* Currant.

Broccoli *see* Cabbage.

Brussels Sprouts *see* Cabbage.

Cabbage All these closely allied crops suffer from the following diseases and pests but the severity of the attacks varies from season to season: club root, cabbage root fly, cabbage whitefly, cabbage white butterfly, cabbage moth and flea beetle.

Cape Gooseberry Inspect the plants weekly for aphids, especially the tips of the shoots and at the stalk ends of the 'lanterns'.

Carrots Aphids and carrot fly are the primary pests. Occasionally powdery and downy mildews, soft rot and root splitting (when drought is followed by heavy rain) can be troublesome. One disease that is easily recognized at lifting is violet root rot, that shows as a web of violet-coloured fungal threads on the outside of the root. Freshly-lifted infected roots are edible peeled, but liable to rot when stored.

Cauliflower These are liable to all the cabbage pests qv.

Celeriac *see* Celery.

Celery Celery is subject to several pests and diseases, notably slugs, celery fly maggots and celery leaf spot fungus.

Cherry Birds are the main pest of cherries, closely followed by the leaf curling aphid known as cherry blackfly. Blossom wilt, spur blight and wither tip (see under Brown rot) are not uncommon especially on morello cherries. Caterpillars of winter moth and cherry fruit moth can sometimes be troublesome. Bacterial canker and silver leaf can also infect trees.

APHIDS Cherry blackfly, that overwinters in the egg stage and hatches at about the time of bud-burst, can be very damaging to cherry trees. Infected leaves curl up and the new growth is severely checked.

CATERPILLARS Winter moth and related caterpillars sometimes attack cherries as the flower-buds open.

CHERRY FRUIT MOTH The caterpillars of this moth bore into the flower-buds and feed on the flowers and young fruitlets.

Below: a serious infestation of cherry blackfly. Below right: leek attacked by rust disease.

CONTROL OF CHERRY PESTS
As with plums and damsons, winter washes give some control of the main pests, but it is easier to rely on a general insecticide, such as malathion, fenitrothion or dimethoate, applied at white-bud stage. Ideally, the selected product should have some systemic activity to control the leaf-curling cherry blackfly.

CHERRY DISEASES
Always cut out diseased wood of the cherry in the summer, thus lessening any risk of further infection.

BACTERIAL CANKER This bacterial disease can be very damaging, as it kills whole branches and can lead to the complete dieback of the tree. Infection occurs during autumn, and the disease then progresses during the winter months. Leaves on infected branches turn yellow and brown.

CONTROL OF CHERRY DISEASES
The recommended method of control for bacterial blight is to give three applications of a copper fungicide – Bordeaux mixture, for example – at two-week intervals, starting in early to mid autumn (end of August). It is also desirable to cut away any badly infected branches.

Cobnut Nut weevil is the most serious pest, while bud rot and nut drop are fairly common diseases.

Courgette If grown under glass, red spider mite can be troublesome. Cucumber mosaic virus can also attack courgettes.

Cucumber Red spider mite and cucumber mosaic virus are the main enemies of the cucumber.

Currants The only serious pests of currants are aphids, and of blackcurrants, gall mites ('big bud' mites).

Damson *see* Plum.

Filbert *see* Cobnut.

Garlic Garlic plants are generally free of pests and diseases.

Gherkin *see* Cucumber.

Globe Artichoke *see* Artichoke.

Gooseberry One serious disease, American gooseberry mildew and three pests, sawfly caterpillar, magpie moth caterpillar and aphids may prove troublesome on gooseberries.

Grape Vines in a greenhouse may be afflicted by mealy bugs and powdery mildew. Grape splitting can also be a problem.

Jerusalem Artichokes *see* Artichokes.

Kale Kales are susceptible to several of the pests and diseases that commonly affect brassicas. *See* Cabbage.

Kohl Rabi *see* Turnips.

Leeks Leeks can be attacked by most onion pests and diseases, notably onion fly, white rot and eelworm. In addition they are subject to attacks by rust disease, which appears as yellow or orange spots. Any leaves showing infection spots should be removed immediately and burned. A programme of regular sprays with a general fungicide should be initiated to protect the plants from further attacks.

Another important disease of leeks is white tip, caused by the fungus *Phytophthora porri*. Normally this disease is restricted to the tips of the leaves, which die and turn white, but it can also affect the edges of the leaves. Caught early, this disease responds to treatment.

Above: a lettuce root attacked by aphids.
Centre: downy mildew on a lettuce.
Right: a plant suffering from onion fly.

At the first sign of the disease the plants should be sprayed with a copper fungicide and repeat applications given at intervals of 14 days during the winter.

Lettuce The main pests to guard against are slugs, birds and aphids. Slug bait will help to keep them down and spraying with a good insecticide will control the greenfly. It is wise to spray occasionally before the hearts have formed, even if no greenfly can be seen, as it is impossible to get at them once the lettuce begins to 'heart up'. Watch out for birds as they can soon ruin a promising crop, sparrows being especially notorious for this. The two main diseases are mosaic disease and grey mould (*botrytis cinerea*).

Outdoor lettuce is normally fairly resistant to disease attack. In overcrowded beds, however, the plants can become infected with a downy mildew. Affected leaves turn patchy yellow and the fungus can be seen on the underside as mealy-looking spots. Since this disease is usually confined to the outer leaves it does little real damage, though heavy infections can spoil the look of the heads. The answer to this disease on outdoor lettuce is to use wide spacings to ensure free air movements around the plants.

Sclerotina disease, which is also called drop, may develop on lettuce in warm weather. The attack begins at ground level, producing a white, fluffy fungal growth that then spreads over the plant, causing it to collapse. Later the fungus produces its small, black, resting bodies (sclerotia) that contaminate the soil. It is therefore important to remove and burn any infected plants as quickly as possible.

Grey mould (botrytis), only occasionally encountered outdoors although very prevalent in the greenhouse, can cause the plants to wilt completely and the leaves to become covered with grey furry mould; spraying regularly with benomyl or thiram will assist in preventing and controlling the disease.

Loganberry *see* Raspberry.

Maize *see* Sweet Corn.

Marrow Red spider mite can be a problem with marrows in particular, while marrows and other cucurbits are all liable to attack by a powdery mildew (cucumber mildew) that can seriously check their growth. This disease can be controlled by spraying with an anti-mildew fungicide. Infection by mosaic virus is also a common problem with cucurbits. This type of virus is readily recognized by the presence of small, puckered leaves showing yellow mottling. Any young plants with these symptoms should be dug up and burnt as they will not produce worthwhile crops. Established plants that become infected in the later growth stages can, however, be left to grow on, but destroy them after the crop is harvested.

Mulberry Mulberry trees are virtually disease-free, but they do occasionally suffer from twig canker. Affected shoots, carrying brownish waxy pustules, should be cut out and burnt as soon as you spot them.

Nectarine *see* Peach.

Onion Onion fly can be a problem while thrips, eelworm, white rot and mildew can only be a nuisance. Downy mildew of onions can be a serious problem in wet seasons. The first sign of attack is the appearance of light-coloured spots on the leaves. These then enlarge and the affected leaves topple over and shrivel. This disease can have serious effects on the crop yield, so the plant should be sprayed with a general fungicide (such as zineb) at the first sign of attack and repeat treatments given at 7–10 day intervals. It is also important to collect and burn any infected leaves in order to reduce the carry-over of disease.

White rot is a common disease of onions that is generally favoured by cool conditions. This disease can be detected by the leaves yellowing and wilting even when there is plenty of soil moisture. If affected plants are closely examined it will be seen that there is a white fluffy growth at the base of the bulbs. This cottony growth later gives rise to small, black, dot-like sclerotia that are the resting bodies of the fungus. These sclerotia fall off into the soil and are then spread around by subsequent cultivations to provide a source of infection in later years. At present there is no cure for infected plants nor is it easy to disinfect the soil. So, once the disease has appeared in an onion bed, the only answer is to practise long-term crop rotation.

Parsnips Parsnips are remarkably free from disease. They may, however, be attacked by downy mildew, powdery mildew and leaf spot. Fortunately these diseases have little effect on the crop.

Far left: aphid effect on peach leaves. Left: peach leaves infested with red spider mite. Above: leaf curl causes peach leaves to swell and distort, and also to redden. Below: powdery growth on the skin of peaches indicates the presence of powdery mildew. Bottom: pea moth maggots can quickly bore their way into developing pods.

Canker (sometimes called 'rust') can, however, be very damaging to the roots. This disease first appears as reddish-brown marks on the top of the root. Later it can lead to a general rot. The easy answer in this case is to sow canker-resistant varieties such as Avonresister. Celery and carrot fly may also attack on occasion.

Peach Bush peach trees are not usually attacked by pests to a degree that warrants spraying, but the fungus disease peach leaf curl must be prevented. Fan-trained trees are vulnerable to aphids and red spider mite. The following pests also affect nectarines and apricots, for which the controls are the same as for peaches.
APHIDS Several species of greenfly and blackfly attack peach trees at bud-burst or shortly after, causing severe leaf curl.
RED SPIDER MITE These small, reddish mites feed on the undersides of the leaves, causing a speckling of the foliage. In severe cases, the leaves may fall early.

CONTROL OF PEACH PEST

Since winter washes are liable to damage some varieties, it is better to rely on spring and summer sprays. A routine spray with a systemic greenfly killer such as malathion, dimethoate or fenitrothion should therefore be applied at the end of the blossom period to deal with greenfly and blackfly. If red spider mite is present, spray against it before flowers open.

PEACH DISEASES

The following diseases also affect nectarines and apricots, and the same controls apply as for peaches.
LEAF CURL This extremely widespread and common disease causes the leaves to thicken and become distorted. Infected leaves also fall prematurely, so the disease has serious effects on the cropping and general vigour of the trees.
POWDERY MILDEW This overwinters in the buds, causing them to produce stunted growth covered with a thick coating of powdery spores that are capable of infecting healthy leaves.

CONTROL OF PEACH DISEASES

The standard recommendation for the control of leaf curl is to spray the trees in early spring (end of February) with either a copper fungicide or lime sulphur. A second spray should be applied in autumn just before leaf fall. An alternative approach is to spray with thiram at fortnightly intervals, starting when the first diseased leaves appear.

Thiram sprays will also help to control powdery mildew, as will a series of sulphur sprays, applied every 14 days, starting when the disease is first noticed.

Pea Both mice and birds are partial to peas and it may also be necessary to combat pea and bean weevil, pea moth, thrips and attacks of mildew. Garden peas are subject to attack by various soil organisms, both at the time of germination and in the later growth stages. Some protection against these diseases can be obtained by the use of captan-based seed dressings, but it is still necessary to practise crop rotation to ensure regular healthy harvests.

Attacks by powdery mildew (that appears as a white powdery covering on leaves and stems) are common in dry summers, particularly on late crops. Anti-mildew sprays (like dinocap) will help to combat this disease: you should also pull out and burn infected plants as soon as they have finished cropping, otherwise they act as sources of infection for later-planted rows.

Pear Most of the pests and diseases of apples attack pears also. The main ones are: brown rot, scab, pear midge, blossom wilt, aphids, capsid, caterpillars, slugworm, canker, honey fungus, phosphorus and potassium deficiencies. They are also susceptible to fireblight. Aphids, capsid, pear sucker and winter moth are all readily controlled by the simple programme of four sprays – at the green cluster stage (when the flower trusses are extending but the flower-buds are still green), the white-bud stage, at petal-fall, and fruitlet stage – as recommended for apples.

CONTROL OF PEAR DISEASES

As with apples, any diseases that attack pears when they are in storage are not included below.

PEAR SCAB This is the principal disease of pears; its symptoms are similar to apple scab. It is controlled by spraying with one of the following – benomyl, captan, sulphur or thiram – when the disease is first noticed.

FIREBLIGHT This is a bacterial disease which causes rapid dieback of infected branches, and cannot be controlled by spray treatments. Some control may be obtained in the early stages of the attack by cutting out and burning infected branches at not less than 60cm (24 in) below the visible signs of the disease. You can check if the disease is present by peeling back the bark – the wood appears reddish brown if it is infected. In Britain, however, statutory regulations under the Fireblight Disease Order require that any outbreak of this disease should be immediately reported to the authorities. Therefore advice should be sought from your local authority as to the best method of controlling the disease.

Pepper Usually free from pests and diseases except for occasional attacks of red spider mite.

Plum The following pests and diseases affect both damsons and plums: aphids, caterpillars, red spider mite, plum fruit moth, plum sawfly, plum rust, silver leaf, blossom wilt and brown rot.

Whether it be damsons or plums, the steps outlined for the control of these pests are the same.

APHIDS Three species of aphid attack plums and damsons, and all overwinter as eggs on the bark. These eggs hatch out at bud-burst, and the young greenfly move on to the new growth. All three species interfere with extension growth, the leaf-curling aphid particularly so.

CATERPILLARS Winter moth and other caterpillars feed on developing foliage.

RED SPIDER MITE Damsons, and some varieties of plum – Czar, for example – are prone to attack by this pest. Red spiders pass the winter as bright red

Top: pear scab produces olive-green blotches on the leaves and dark brown calluses on the mature fruits. Above: aphids swarming over a plum tree.

eggs on the bark, and hatch out in early summer (May). The small, reddish-coloured mites feed on the undersides of the leaves, causing them to become speckled and sometimes bronzed. In certain cases, the leaves may fall prematurely.
PLUM FRUIT MOTH Adult moths lay their eggs at the base of the fruit stalk from late summer to early autumn (mid July to early August). The developing caterpillars eat their way to the fruit stone, where they mature, and then – in early to mid autumn (late August) – they depart to complete their development. When mature the caterpillars are reddish in colour, hence their name of red plum maggots.
PLUM SAWFLY The adults lay eggs on the flowers during blossoming, and the creamy white caterpillars then live on the fruits till they are mature, when they drop to the ground to pupate.

CONTROL OF PLUM PESTS

Winter washes are some help against aphids and red spider mite, but a simpler, easier approach is to rely on spring and summer sprays. Normally all that is needed for the effective control of aphids and caterpillars is a routine spray at white-bud stage with a good garden insecticide such as malathion, fenitrothion or dimethoate. Ideally, the spray should show some systemic activity in order to control leaf-curling aphids.

If plum sawfly is a problem, then you will have to give a second spray at petal fall, but in most cases this will be enough. However, if red spider mite appears, it will also be necessary to spray in mid summer (early June), and again two or three weeks later.

Finally, an attack by plum fruit moth will mean further sprays in late summer

and again in early autumn (late July and mid August).

PLUM DISEASES

The following diseases also affect damsons; treatment is the same as for plums.
BLOSSOM WILT AND BROWN ROT This overwinters in cankers and in mummified fruits. These infection centres then produce spores in spring that infect the blossoms, causing them to wilt. The same disease is responsible, later in the season, for a brown rot of the fruits.
PLUM RUST Small brown spots on the underside of the leaves and a speckling of the upper leaf surfaces are the indications of this disease.
SILVER LEAF A fungus enters the wood through a wound, causing a silvering of the leaves and dieback of the shoots.
CONTROL OF PLUM DISEASES
Cutting out cankered wood – painting the wounds with a sealing paint – and collecting and burning mummified fruits is the best way to deal with blossom wilt and brown rot. Should plum rust develop, however, protective sprays with thiram or zineb should be applied to reduce the spread of the disease.

In the case of silver leaf, cut out infected shoots and burn them, and paint the wounds with protective paint.

Potato The most frequently-encountered enemies of the potato are potato blight,

Above: potato tuber rotted with blight, the best known of potato diseases.
Left: the small brown spots on the underside of these plum leaves point to infestation of rust disease. The spread of this disease can be controlled by protective sprays of thiram or zineb.
Far left: prominent among the pests which affect the plum are caterpillars, which burrow through to the fruit stone.

common scab and potato eelworm.

Potato blight blackens the leaves and can lead to rotting of the tubers. To control this disease, spray at the first sign of attack with a copper fungicide and follow this with two or three repeat treatments at 14-day intervals. Finally cut off, remove and burn the haulm 7–10 days before lifting the crop in order to prevent infection of the tubers.

Virus diseases are another major cause of crop reduction. These infections are detected by the yellow mottling, rolling or crinkling of the foliage. Much the best insurance against virus diseases is to buy fresh certified seed potatoes each year.

Common scab is a widely-spread disease. This produces blemishes on the surface of the tubers but otherwise has no ill effects. Incorporating plenty of bulky organic matter into the drill at planting time reduces the incidence of common scab. It is also important not to lime the soil before planting potatoes.

Quince Quince trees may suffer from leaf blight.

Radish Flea beetle and birds are the main enemies of the radish grower.

Raspberry Raspberries are prone to botrytis and also virus infections notably raspberry mosaic.

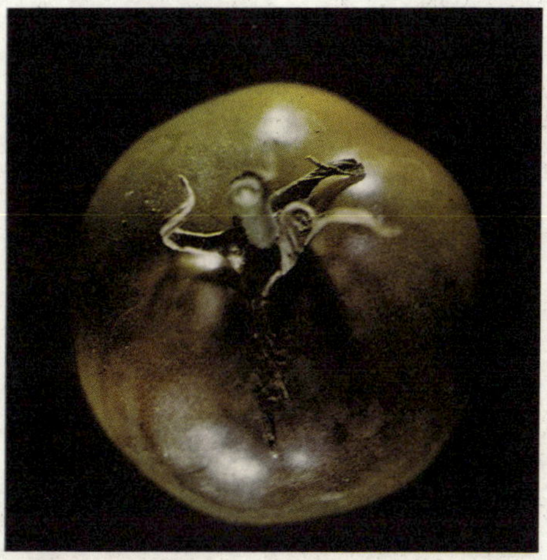

Above: radishes and turnips are susceptible to the ravages of the flea beetle. Above right: tomato with buck-eye rot, a disease carried by soil-borne fungi. It takes the form of dark patches, with darker concentric circles, at the end of the fruit, opposite to the stalk. Far right: yellow and brown discoloration of tomato foliage is indicative of leaf mould, prevalent in hot, dry weather.

Redcurrant *see* Currants.

Rhubarb The only calamity likely to affect rhubarb is crown rot.

Shallot Shallots may sometimes be attacked by the onion fly or by onion white rot disease, but such attacks are not common. For the most part they are easy to grow and trouble free.

Spinach The black bean aphid is a primary pest of spinach and spinach beet. Usually less troublesome are downy mildew, leaf miner and leaf spot.

Sprouts *see* Cabbage.

Strawberry Strawberries fall prey to many pests, but most of them are easily controlled. Leaf spot, red core, mildew and grey mould (botrytis) are fungus diseases which may attack strawberries. There are also several types of virus diseases that attack these plants. The superficial symptoms of these diseases are very similar – stunting of the plant and discoloration of the leaves.

Swede *see* Turnip.

Sweet Corn The only pest likely to be bothersome is frit fly. Occasionally smut disease and boron deficiency may occur.

Sweet Peppers *see* Peppers.

Tomato The modern tomato is a highly developed plant and as such is subject to various diseases – most of them occurring in the fruiting stage. However, if you raise and tend your plants carefully, you should be able to harvest a healthy crop without difficulty. The more common troubles that can occur include: potato blight, leaf mould, blossom-end rot, greenback, split fruits, leaf curl and red spider mite.

Potato blight is a major disease of outdoor tomatoes; it not only damages the leaves but also causes a black rot of the fruits. Here again the use of regular sprays with a copper fungicide is recommended to prevent this.

Various soil-borne fungi can cause damping off of seedlings and foot rots of older plants. Foot rot is a very general term used to describe various diseases, all due to fungi of one sort or another, that reveal themselves as a blackening and rotting of the plants.

One of these soil-borne fungi, *Phytophthora parasitica*, is also responsible for buck-eye rot of the fruits. This takes the form of dark patches, with darker concentric rings, at the end of the fruit opposite to the stalk. Watering the soil with Cheshunt compound or captan fungicide is the best way of guarding against these diseases. Another fruit blemish that is similar to buck-eye rot but has no concentric rings, is called blossom-end rot. This trouble, however, is not caused by disease but is produced by water shortages at an earlier stage of development.

As with potatoes, tomatoes can also be infected by a variety of virus diseases that cause leaf discoloration and growth distortion. There is no cure for these diseases, but they can often be prevented by controlling the aphids that frequently transmit the infection.

In a hot dry summer, leaf mould disease may be a nuisance. The leaves develop yellow patches on the upper surface and a brownish mould beneath. Spray at regular 10–14 day intervals with a copper fungicide, used according to manufacturer's instructions.

Turnip The main enemies of turnips are the flea beetle and a condition resulting from boron deficiency. Swedes and turnips can also be attacked by the diseases listed under brassicas. They may be attacked by powdery mildew, but this disease does not usually have very serious effects. In addition the roots can be attacked by various root rots. Dry rot shows itself by sunken, cankerous areas appearing on the side of the root. Soft rot may enter through these wounds or where mechanical damage has taken place. This turns the roots to a slimy mass, often leaving the skin almost intact. Brown rot turns the flesh of the root dark brown or black. There are no specific control measures for these root diseases, but any infected plants that are discovered should be destroyed.

Walnut Bacterial blight can be a problem in some areas.

Watercress On the whole, watercress is remarkably free of pests and diseases. Downy mildew, leaf spot and mosaic virus may give local infections.

Whitecurrant *see* Currants.

Zucchini *see* Marrow.

PRIMULA
PROLIFERA

A-Z WEEDS AND THEIR CONTROL

Bellflower, creeping Botanically known as *Campanula rapunculoides,* this is an example of a garden plant becoming a weed. Above ground it produces 60cm (2 ft) tall spikes of purple bells, each about 3cm (1 in) long, and narrow, heart-shaped, toothed leaves. A clump in full bloom is most attractive. Underground if forms fleshy, white, carrot-like roots and far spreading underground stems. All parts of the root system produce new stems and spread is rapid.

CONTROL Once established, this plant is difficult to eradicate. Digging out the main root system is the best beginning, then continually hoeing out all young shoots that form. Glyphosate gives some control if used several times.

Bindweed Also known as bellbind and other less complimentary names; two distinct entities go under this name. Field bindweed (*Convolvulus arvensis*) rarely grows above 90cm (3 ft) tall, has triangular leaves to 5cm (2 in) long and pink, white, or pink and white widely funnel-shaped flowers 2·5cm (1 in) wide. Hedge bindweed (*Calystegia sepium*) and the similar larger bindweed (*C. sylvatica*) grow to 3m (10 ft) or so with leaves to 10cm (4 in) or more long and trumpet-shaped white flowers 5–7·5cm (2–3 in) wide. All have very deeply delving roots which spread underground and send up new stems. The latter are wiry and spiral tightly around the nearest support.

CONTROL Regularly digging out all stems that show with as much root as possible weakens the plant, but several years are needed to eliminate all the roots. Dichlobenil and glyphosate are worth using, though even these otherwise efficient herbicides will need to be used several times, ideally as a gel brushed on the leaves.

Bittercress, hairy This tiny annual plant, botanically *Cardamine hirsuta,* is one of the most ubiquitous of all garden weeds and is a real curse in garden centres and nurseries. It forms rosettes of narrow leaves, each technically pinnate and formed of about 5–15 small leaflets. The white flowers are four-petalled and very small, carried in short spikes. The narrow seed-pods explode when ripe, showering seeds up to 90cm (3 ft) away. Depending on the soil and site, plants can be 3–5cm (1–2 in) high and wide or several times larger. In poor soils the plants are tiny and flower in a few weeks of germination. Thus several generations of this plant occur during each growing season. An average-sized plant can produce about 600 seeds.

CONTROL Regular hoeing has much to recommend it, making sure that not a single plant is allowed to seed. Several herbicides are also efficient killers, including simazine, dichlobenil and glyphosate. Propachlor will prevent seeds germinating.

Bracken In Britain, bracken (*Pteridium aquilinum*) is the only fern classifiable as a weed. Unlike most popular ferns, bracken has fast-creeping, deeply seated stems or rhizomes which produce, at intervals, single, long-stalked leaves or

Below: hedge bindweed.

Above: bracken is the only fern to be classified as a weed. Right: the lesser celandine is technically a buttercup. Below right: the meadow buttercup.

fronds, usually 45–80cm (18–32 in) tall.
CONTROL Preventing the plant from maturing its leaves weakens the rhizomes and eventually kills them. If possible, first dig out the rhizomes then regularly break off all fronds as they emerge. The herbicide glyphosate gives a reasonable control.

Buttercup Among several species of native *Ranunculus*, only creeping buttercup (*R. repens*) is a widespread nuisance. Rapidly covering the soil with its strawberry-like runners and dissected, trifoliate leaves it also produces abundant seed which germinates readily. If not caught in time it soon infiltrates into the centres of suckering shrubs, hardy perennials and rock plants and is then difficult to remove. On rich moist soil one plant can spread over an area of 4 sq m (5 sq yd) in a single year.
CONTROL As all the growth is at or above soil level this weed can be removed by turning it under when digging one spit deep. Hoeing is also efficient providing the roots are severed beneath the runners. It is also susceptible to 2,4–D, MCPA, paraquat and diquat.

Celandine, lesser Botanically *Ranunculus ficaria,* the lesser celandine is technically a buttercup. It is the only other member of its genus in Britain to behave as a weed but is only troublesome locally. Celandine is a tufted perennial with tuberous-roots and long-stalked, heart-shaped leaves and buttercup-like flowers with about eight narrow yellow petals. There are two forms of this plant, one with bulbils in the leaf axils, one without. The former is usually the garden weed.

Growth begins in late winter and the weed dies away completely by mid summer, so it has short-term nuisance-value.
CONTROL Forking out when in full leaf is very effective on light soils, more difficult on clay ones. Care must be taken not to break up the tuber clusters as each one can form a new plant. Where convenient, the herbicides 2,4–D, MCPA, paraquat and diquat are effective.

Chickweed This bright green, mat-forming annual or biennial with its small oval, pointed leaves and tiny off-white flowers is one of the commonest weeds and familiar even to non-gardeners. Botanically it is *Stellaria media.*
CONTROL Young plants hoe out easily and soon die if the weather is warm and dry. Larger mats can be skimmed off with a spade or buried during digging operations. Chickweed is susceptible to all the commonly available herbicides.

Cleavers Commonly known also as goosegrass and sweethearts, *Galium aparine* can be a real curse among ornamental shrubs and border perennials. It is an annual climber with wiry, angular stems and whorls of narrow leaves. The whole plant is covered with minute hooks, enabling it to stick to any rough surface and climb to 2m (6 ft) or more. Minute, off-white four-petalled flowers give rise to pairs of hooked seeds (technically fruits).
CONTROL Hand pulling is the best way of removing the long, straggling stems. It is not a very efficient means of eradication as they break easily and re-growth appears. If done before seeding, however, it does prevent the next year's

Left: white clover Trifolium repens *spreads vigorously. Above: the daisy is a perennial weed. Right: broad-leaved dock* (Rumex obtusifolius).

crop. Seedlings can be hoed off easily. Where herbicides can be used, mecoprop, propachlor and dichlobenil are useful killers.

Clover White clover (*Trifolium repens*) and lesser trefoil (*T. dubium*) are both weeds of lawns. White clover can also be a nuisance in flower beds. It has fast creeping stems and long-stalked, trifoliate leaves. The globular clusters of small flowers are white. Lesser trefoil is a smaller, much-branched plant with wiry stems, short-stalked trifoliate leaves and tiny yellow flowers in stalked clusters.
CONTROL White clover stands mowing well and can be used as a substitute lawn in dry areas. To kill it in a grass lawn one of the following herbicides must be used, dicamba, fenoprop, mecoprop or dichlorprop. 2,4–D and MCPA have little or no effect, but they do kill lesser trefoil.

Coltsfoot Starting to bloom in later winter before its leaves, coltsfoot (*Tussilago farfara*) is a real harbinger of spring by roadsides and on waste ground. In the garden, however, it can be a troublesome weed with its brittle underground stems and large leaves. The latter are up to 20cm (8 in) or more wide, shallowly lobed and white-felted beneath. The showy, yellow, dandelion-like flowers are carried on purplish, woolly and scaly stems.
CONTROL Digging out all that is possible of the root system is recommended followed by regular hoeing as the rhizome fragments produce leaves. Most herbicides are not very effective but dichlobenil and glyphosate are promising.

Couch grass, *see* Grasses.

Daisy The common or lawn daisy (*Bellis perennis*) is known to all as a perennial lawn weed. In some soils it seeds into borders but is rarely a nuisance. The familiar white daisy flower heads, which may or may not be carmine tinted in bud, close each evening.
CONTROL If a perfect grass sward is wanted, common daisy is susceptible to most lawn weedkillers.

Dandelion Like the common daisy, the dandelion is familiar to all and needs no description. Even so, it is a very variable plant in stature, flower size and leaf toothing or lobing. The common species comes under *Taraxacum officinale,* but three other species can be confused with it and there are dozens of microspecies.
CONTROL As root fragments regenerate vigorously, digging an established plant is largely a waste of time. Small plants can usually be removed entirely. The herbicide, 2,4–D is very effective in lawns and can be painted on the leaves of dandelions in ornamental borders. Dichlobenil is also good.

Deadnettle Deadnettles must not be confused with the true nettles. Botanically members of the genus *Lamium,* they belong to the same family (*Labiatae*) as sage and entirely lack stinging hairs. The tubular, two-lipped flowers are quite showy. The annual red deadnettle (*L. purpureum*) and its close ally, henbit (*L. amplexicaule*), both with pinkish-purple flowers, can be a nuisance in the garden especially among vegetables. The white deadnettle (*Lamium album*) is only occasionally a serious weed. A perennial, it spreads by underground stems and soon colonises a border of shrubs or hardy perennials if not curbed.
CONTROL Hand pulling and hoeing are both very effective. White deadnettle must be forked out, then treated with a herbicide. The only herbicides that will give good control are simazine, propachlor and glyphosate.

Docks The spire-like seeding stems of docks are a familiar sight by roadsides and on waste land. Two distinct sorts are

sometimes a nuisance in neglected gardens. Broad-leaved dock (*Rumex obtusifolius*) has broadly lance-shaped leaves up to 25cm (10 in) long. Curled dock (*R. crispus*) has lance-shaped leaves of similar length with strongly waved or crisped margins. Both are deep rooted perennials with tiny greenish or reddish flowers and winged, triangular seeds (botanically fruits).
CONTROL Digging out with a spade is the quickest method. Providing the top 15cm (6 in) of the tap root is removed there will be no regeneration. Seedlings must be hoed off when young. It is important to prevent plants from seeding. A large plant can produce as many as 30,000 seeds a year and at least some of these can survive under the soil for up to 80 years. Among herbicides, dichlobenil and glyphosate are the most efficient, 2,4–D can be used in grassland.

Fat hen More conspicuous on farmland, but not infrequent as a garden weed, fat hen (*Chenopodium album*) is a quick-growing annual weed. From about 30–90cm (1–3 ft) in height, it is an erect plant often with only a few branches. The leaves are oval to roughly triangular in outline and have a silvery cast. The minute, petalless flowers are borne in clusters from the leaf axils. There are several allied species of *Chenopodium* known as goosefoot. They resemble fat hen in a general sort of way but are usually greener and more branched. They are only rarely troublesome weeds.
CONTROL Hoeing when young and hand pulling when older are efficient, age-old methods. The following herbicides are effective: chloroxuron, paraquat/diquat, 2,4–D, simazine, dichlorbenil.

Fleabane, Canadian Essentially a plant of neglected gardens and waste land, Canadian fleabane (*Conyza canadensis*) is only locally a troublesome weed. Behaving as both annual and biennial, it is an erect, thin, hairy plant, 30–90cm (1–3 ft) tall. The leaves are narrowly lance-shaped and the tiny, groundsel-like flower-heads are white. This plant was introduced from North America about 1700.
CONTROL Hoeing and hand pulling are efficient and the plant is susceptible to 2,4–D, MCPA, glyphosate.

Above: common fumitory. Above right: couch grass (Agropyron repens).

Fumitory Botanically known as *Fumaria,* the various sorts of fumitory are rarely so abundant as to be real nuisance weeds. The commonest fumitory is *F. officinalis.* It is a bushy plant 20–40cm (8–16 in) tall with finely dissected greyish, fern-like leaves and short spikes of quaint, tubular pink flowers.
CONTROL Hoeing is an easy and efficient method, or the following herbicides can be used: chlorpropham, 2, 4–D, simazine.

Gallant soldier This localized weed arrived in Britain from S. America about 1870. It is an erect plant 20–60cm (8–24 in) tall which may or may not be well-branched, with oval, toothed, pointed leaves about 3–5cm (1–2 in) long. The tiny flower heads are somewhat daisy-like but with only five very small white ray florets. The common gallant soldier (*Galinsoga parviflora*) is hairless; the otherwise very similar *G. ciliata* is hairy.
CONTROL Hoeing, hand pulling and use of most herbicides are effective methods.

Goosefoot *see* Fat hen.

Goosegrass *see* Cleavers.

Grasses Several different grass species can be serious weeds in the garden. The commonest of these is annual meadow grass (*Poa annua*). It is usually a small, tufted plant under 15cm (6 in) tall, but occasionally reaches twice this height. It flowers freely, often when very small, the tiny yellowish green spikelets being borne in loose, terminal clusters. In some gardens two or three perennial meadow grasses can be a nuisance. Rough meadow grass (*P. trivialis*) and smooth meadow grass, (*P. pratensis*) are similar to each other, both reaching about 60cm (2 ft) in flower. Both have creeping stems, those of *P. pratensis* underground. One of the worst perennial grasses with deeply delving, far-spreading underground stems (rhizomes) is couch or twitch (*Agropyron repens*). This grass is easily identified by its wheat-like flowering spikes and long, wiry rhizomes. Barren brome grass (*Bromus* (*Anisantha*) *sterilis*) is an annual or biennial species to 60cm (2 ft) or more tall. It has a loosely tufted habit, softly hairy leaves and airy clusters of drooping, flowering spikelets tipped with long bristles (awns). It is a plant of light soils and is sometimes troublesome in neglected gardens.
CONTROL The annual species can be easily hoed out when young. The perennials are best if as much as possible is forked out first, then treated with a herbicide such as dalapon, paraquat/diquat and simazine. The new alloydium-sodium is an excellent specific cure for couch grass.

Ground elder This familiar weed can be a serious problem under certain conditions.

Ground elder (*Aegopodium podagraria*) has fast-growing, brittle, white underground stems from which arise tufts of leaves. The latter are compound, each composed of three to nine oval leaflets. The tiny white flowers are carried in flat-topped clusters on erect, leafy stems 60cm (2 ft) or more tall.
CONTROL For those who have the time and energy and who garden on light soils, digging out the rhizomes is very worthwhile. On clay soils these underground stems fragment easily, making it difficult to remove them cleanly. The herbicides dichlobenil, 2,4,5–T and glyphosate are all worth trying, the last named being the most efficient.

Groundsel Botanically *Senecio vulgaris*, groundsel is a ubiquitous weed which even most non-gardeners can identify with its somewhat fleshy-lobed leaves and cylindrical 'petalless' flowering heads (There is also an uncommon form, *S. vulgaris radiatus*, which has flower heads with short, yellow ray petals).
CONTROL Hoeing is effective but air-borne seeds soon re-colonize bare soil. The following herbicides are effective: propachlor, chloroxuron, glyphosate, simazine and dichlobenil.

Horsetail, field Although it is not a common garden weed, when field horsetail (*Equisetum arvense*) does occur it can be a serious problem. The horsetails are primitive plants which are allied to the ferns and reproduce by spores. Many of the species, field horsetail included, have deeply delving rhizomes which are almost impossible to eradicate. The stems are tubular, erect, with whorls of slender, jointed, green stems that look like grassy leaves. In field horsetail, the spores are borne in small, cone-like structures terminating short, brownish, unbranched stems in spring.
CONTROL Dichlobenil, if applied early each year, will eventually kill out this weed. Sodium chlorate, where it can be used, gives some control.

Knotgrass Common knotgrass (*Polygonum aviculare*) is often a nuisance on paths and sometimes in beds and borders. An annual, it forms mats of prostrate, very tough, wiry stems clad with lance-shaped leaves about 2·5cm (1 in) long. The white or pink-tinted tiny flowers occur in small clusters in the leaf axils.
CONTROL Hoeing at the seedling stage is effective, but once the stems age and toughen it becomes hard work. Glyphosate, simazine and paraquat/diquat all give fairly good control.

Knotweed, Japanese Once cultivated as an ornamental, Japanese knotweed (*Polygonum cuspidatum*) is now rarely planted, though it is not infrequent on railway banks and by roadsides. It is a thicket-forming plant 2–3m (6–10 ft) tall with erect, almost woody, bamboo-like stems clad with big oval leaves to 15cm (6 in) or more long. Sprays of small white flowers open in autumn.
CONTROL Established colonies are difficult to remove entirely. The best plan is to dig out with mattock and spade as much as possible, ideally when in full summer growth. From then on treat all leafy shoots that regenerate with glyphosate.

Lichen These curious and unique plants, formed by the fusion of a fungus and an alga, are not harmful, though on fruit trees some people consider them unsightly. The flat, pale brown to grey, frond-like growths of dog lichen on lawns indicates a soil that is too poor for good grass, especially one which is too acid or sandy.
CONTROL Raking, spiking, top-dressing and regular feeding will eliminate it and encourage the grass to thicken. To clean up trees, spray with tar oil winter wash.

Liverwort Primitive spore-bearing plant, together with the mosses forming the order *Bryophyta*. There are two sorts: **1** foliose, somewhat moss-like with thread-like creeping stems and tiny leaves;

Below: common liverwort Marchantia polymorpha. *Bottom: the lichen* Peltigera canina *forms dense unsightly clumps.*

2 thallose, leafless, the stems ribbon-like, usually branched or lobed. The latter group is often represented in gardens by common liverwort (*Marchantia polymorpha*), which can form extensive bright green patches where conditions are constantly moist and the light diffused. It can be a nuisance on pot plants and assume pest proportions when long-term germinating seed is plunged outside.
CONTROL There is no easy remedy and the flattened stems should be skimmed off as soon as recognized. Seed pots are best kept dark under asbestos or black polythene sheeting; where leaching by rain is necessary to break seed dormancy, a layer of grit or fine gravel should be applied.

Mayweed Two very similar but botanically distinct plants go under the name of mayweed. Scented mayweed or wild chamomile is *Matricaria recutita* and the scentless mayweed is *Tripleurospermum maritimum inodorum*. Both are bushy plants rarely above 30cm (1 ft) tall with very finely dissected leaves and white daisy flowers, but they are rarely serious weeds in gardens. Very similar in foliage but smelling of pineapples and with flowerheads lacking ray petals is the rayless mayweed or pineapple weed (*Matricaria matricarioides*). It can be a nuisance in neglected gardens, especially on paths.
CONTROL Hoeing young plants and hand pulling larger ones is effective if there are not very many. Among efficient herbicides are simazine, dichlobenil, propachlor and glyphosate.

Medick, black With its branched, wiry stems, trifoliate leaves and yellow flowers in tight clusters, black medick (*Medicago lupulina*) resembles lesser trefoil (see Clover). It is mainly a weed of neglected lawns, paths and drives, and is sometimes found in beds and borders.
CONTROL The herbicide mixtures sold as lawn weedkillers are effective but need applying annually, as the long-lived seeds germinate each spring or autumn.

Mosses Several species of moss occur naturally in grassland and multiply under poor soil and close mowing conditions. When they get thick they tend to smother out the grasses and are best removed in late spring.
CONTROL Lawns that are shady or stay very moist as well as those on poor soil all tend to be extra mossy. Removing the shade, improving the drainage and increasing soil fertility are all basic ways of reducing moss. An annual scarifying with a wire-tined rake will also thin down the moss. The following herbicides are used as moss killers: ammonium and ferrous sulphate (mixed with sand and known as lawn sand), calomel or mercurous chloride, chloroxuron, dichlorophen and tar oil.

Mouse-ear In gardens, common mouse-ear (*Cerastium holosteoides* (*fontanum*)) is mainly a weed of lawns though it can occur in beds and borders. It is a semi-prostrate perennial with slender stems and pairs of broadly lance-shaped leaves 1–2·5cm ($\frac{1}{2}$–1 in), long set, with erect, whitish hairs. The tiny off-white flowers have five petals, each one of which is cleft down the middle.
CONTROL All the modern herbicides designed for lawns are effective against this weed. Elsewhere it can be eliminated with simazine, dichlobenil or the hoe.

Nettles The common stinging nettle (*Urtica dioica)* is an over-familiar perennial weed mainly found in neglected gardens, waste ground and disturbed woodland. It has yellowish roots and creeping over- and underground stems. The erect flowering stems can exceed 1.5m (5 ft) in height but are usually less. Minute green flowers open in frothy clusters from the upper leaf axils. The annual nettle (*U. urens*) is smaller in all its parts, lacks the creeping stems and has white roots. Stinging hairs and the minute flowers easily distinguish these true nettles from the deadnettles, qv
CONTROL If only a few plants are present they are best dug out. Large

Below: the common stinging nettle.

Above: the small white flowers of the black nightshade, a common garden weed, are exactly like those of the potato plant. Right: nipplewort (Lapsana communis) *flowers July-September in hedgerows and waste places.*

colonies can be sprayed with a brushwood killer containing 2,4,5-T, or this substance mixed with 2,4-D. Dichlobenil and glyphosate are also efficient. Annual nettle seedlings are easily hoed out.

Nightshade, black A common weed of cultivated ground but seldom a real nuisance, black nightshade (*Solanum nigrum*) is an unlikely relative of the tomato. It is a bushy annual 15–45cm (6–18 in) or so tall, with alternate oval leaves having irregularly toothed or shallow lobed leaves. Pendant, starry white flowers with a central cone of yellow stamens open in lateral clusters between or opposite the leaves. Globular pea-sized berries follow which may turn black or stay greenish, when ripe. They are poisonous but by no means deadly.
CONTROL Hoeing young plants and hand pulling older ones is an easy means of control. The only herbicides worth trying are chloroxuron, simazine, glyphosate and the paraquat/diquat mixture.

Nightshade, enchanter's Enchanter's nightshade (*Circaea lutetiana*) is in no way related to the true nightshade. It does in fact, belong to the family which contains fuchsia and evening primrose (the *Onagraceae*). It is a perennial with far-creeping, white, underground stems (rhizomes). The erect flowering stems bear oval, slender-pointed leaves 4–7.5cm (1½–3 in) long and terminate in slender spikes of tiny white flowers. The latter are curious in having two deeply-cleft petals only. Each flower is followed by a tiny pear-shaped fruit covered with hooked bristles.
CONTROL Carefully digging out the rhizomes is the best way to tackle this plant, though not easy on heavy soils. So far, few of the herbicides have been tried on it, but glyphosate seems promising.

Nipplewort The tall, slender nipplewort (*Lapsana communis*) is very much a weed of waste places and neglected gardens. It is an annual 60–120cm (2–4 ft) tall with small yellow flowerheads, like those of a hawkweed or tiny dandelion, in open-branched terminal clusters. The leaves are technically pinnately lobed but this is not always obvious as the terminal leaflet is very much larger than the rest. The upper leaves are apparently simple and broadly oval, with or without small lobes on the stalk.
CONTROL Hoeing and hand pulling are easy, the latter only if the plant is grasped low down. Paraquat/diquat, glyphosate and most other herbicides are effective killers of nipplewort.

Orache Common orache (*Atriplex patula*) is sometimes confused with fat hen, but it has leaves that are triangular in outline and the plant is generally bushier. It is more a plant of wasteland than gardens, particularly near the sea, but can be a nuisance in neglected beds.
CONTROL Common orache can be controlled in the same way as fat hen, qv

Oxalis This genus contains some highly decorative rock plants and also several pernicious weeds. Yellow-flowered oxalis or procumbent yellow sorrel (*Oxalis corniculata*) is the best known. It is a fibrous-rooted perennial forming mats of pale green trifoliate leaves and bearing five-petalled yellow flowers in groups of one to four from spring to autumn. A miniature form of this is also a nuisance, (*O. exilis*).

Several bulbiliferous species originally introduced as garden plants have become serious weeds. Pink-flowered are *O. corymbosa* and *O. latifolia*. Both are clump-forming to about 15cm (6 in) tall with long-stalked clover-like leaves and a mass of showy, funnel-shaped flowers. Numerous small bulbils crowd around the base of each plant and are easily detached and spread around. *O. incarnata* is similar but spreads into loose hummocks and bears bulbils below ground and on stems above. The flowers are lilac-white and almost translucent.
CONTROL Removing complete plants of the perennial species carefully to avoid spreading the bulbils is a first requisite. Thereafter hoeing and digging out every tiny plant is essential. Even then the long-lived bulbils are quite likely to appear for several years after soil disturbance. The new herbicide oxadiazon is promising but at present is not commercially available. Yellow-flowered sorrel responds to hoeing and the following herbicides: paraquat/diquat, dichlobenil and glyphosate.

Pearlwort The flat, mossy patches of pearlwort (*Sagina procumbens*) are familiar in a variety of garden situations from lawns to flower beds, particularly where moist. It is an extremely annoying perennial weed to those who grow plants in peat beds. The plant is formed of interlacing, thread-like stems clad with equally narrow leaves. Minute flowers which may or may not have four white petals are borne just above the foliage. Annual pearlwort (*S. apetala*) is similar but has a looser, semi-erect habit and petals so tiny as to appear non-existent.
CONTROL In lawns, all the proprietary weedkillers formulated as lawn weed killers are effective against pearlwort.

Elsewhere, dichlobenil and simazine can be used.

Persicaria, pale Pale persicaria (*Polygonum lapathifolium)* is an annual largely confined to cultivated ground and waste places. When abundant it can be a nuisance. It is an erect plant to 60cm (2 ft) or more, though usually less, with green stems and lance-shaped, 5–10cm (2–4 in) long leaves, often with a blackish blotch. The tiny pink flowers are borne in terminal spikes. Very similar but less abundant and with red stems is redshank or willow weed (*P. persicaria)*.
CONTROL Hoeing when young and hand pulling later is effective. Paraquat/diquat, simazine and glyphosate all give control.

Pineapple weed, *see* Mayweed.

Plantains Two species of plantains are associated with waste ground, drives and paths and in neglected gardens they can colonize beds and borders. Ribwort plantain (*Plantago lanceolata*) has rosettes of strongly ribbed, lance-shaped leaves to 15cm (6 in) or more long. The tiny flowers are brownish, borne in short, dense spikes on long naked stems. Greater plantain (*P. major*) has broadly oval leaves in flattened rosettes and elongated green flower spikes. It is sometimes a nuisance in lawns and also appears in flower beds.
CONTROL Hoeing seedlings and young plants is effective. In lawns, 2,4-D, MCPA, dichlorprop and mecoprop (all used in lawn herbicides) will destroy these weeds. Elsewhere, glyphosate can be recommended.

Poppy The common annual poppy (*Papaver rhoeas)* is more a weed of arable farmland than gardens, but on light soils it can sometimes be mildly troublesome in beds and borders. It starts off by forming rosettes of deeply lobed, hairy leaves, then sends up branched stems each bearing a scarlet flower with black anthers. The well-liked 'Shirley' poppy is a colour mixture derived from this species.
CONTROL Hoeing when young is easy and hand pulling later, before the seed is shed. Several herbicides are effective including chloroxuron, chlorpropam and paraquat/diquat.

Top right: the heart-shaped fruits of shepherd's purse give the plant its name. Above and top: the field poppy disperses its seed at intervals through the small openings at the top of its capsule.

Ribwort, *see* Plantains.

Self-heal Medicinal herb and wild flower, self-heal (*Prunella vulgaris)* can also be a weed, mainly of lawns. Semi-prostrate, it forms mats of 2.5–5cm (1–2 in) long oval leaves. Tubular, hooded, violet flowers are carried in short, dense spikes at the top of leafy stems to about 15cm (6 in) tall, but often less.
CONTROL All the reputable herbicide mixtures sold as lawn weedkillers are effective.

Shepherd's purse The heart-shaped seed pods of shepherd's purse (*Capsella bursa-pastoris)* easily proclaim this very common weed. During the summer, especially on poorer soils, the growth cycle can be as short as six weeks. Autumn germinations usually overwinter as rosettes, blooming the following spring. The narrow leaves are jaggedly lobed in a variety of ways, the largest basal ones being the most variable. Leafy flowering stems, 15–45cm (6–18 in) tall, bear spikes of tiny, four-petalled off-white flowers.
CONTROL Carried out during the seedling stage, hoeing is recommended, but later the root toughens. A variety of herbicides can be used, including simazine, dichlobenil, chloroxuron and propachlor.

Sow-thistle As with shepherd's purse, groundsel and dandelion, sow-thistles are weeds that every garden is heir to at one time or another. Smooth or common sow-thistle (*Sonchus oleraceus)* is an erect annual 30–120cm (1–4 ft) tall depending on soil and situation. The basal rosette leaves are pinnately, jaggedly lobed and somewhat greyish. The stem leaves have fewer lobes and broadly

Above: sun spurge (Euphorbia helioscopia). *Right: the germander speedwell* (Veronica chamaedrys). *Below right: petty spurge* (Euphorbia peplus).

winged stalks. If allowed to get large enough the stem tips branch and bear pale yellow flower heads rather like small dandelions. When broken, all parts of the plant exude a white sap. Prickly sow-thistle (*S. asper*) is basically similar but the leaf margins are waved and bear prickle-tipped teeth. Perennial or corn sow-thistle (*S. arvensis*) has far-creeping underground stems and large basal leaves somewhat like those of smooth sow-thistle. The flower heads, however, are much larger, to 4cm (1½ in) wide and the stalks that bear them are covered with yellow, glandular hairs.

CONTROL The annuals can be hoed out when young. Later they can be treated with such herbicides as simazine, dichlobenil, paraquat/diquat and propachlor. Perennial sow-thistle is more difficult to eradicate. Dichlobenil is the best herbicide and glyphosate is worth trying. 2,4-D and MCPA work fairly well if painted on the leaves.

Speedwells Several annual and one perennial speedwell are frequent garden and field weeds. Common field speedwell (*Veronica persica*) is a prostrate annual plant with small, oval, boldly toothed leaves and bright blue and white flowers borne singly in their axils. Wall speedwell (*V. arvensis*) is erect, with spikes of smaller, deep blue flowers. Slender speedwell (*V. filiformis*) is mainly a perennial weed of lawns, though it does invade beds and borders. It forms mats of threadlike stems set with small round leaves having notched margins. The solitary flowers are pale blue and carried in profusion. This is a most attractive speedwell which was originally introduced as a garden plant but soon proved too invasive.

CONTROL Annual species can be easily hoed out or sprayed with paraquat/diquat. Older plants are partially resistant. Propachlor or chlorpropam prevent seeds germinating. Slender speedwell can be eradicated with a mixture of ioxynil and mecoprop. Small infestations can be dealt with using tar oil or by applying lawn sand.

Spurges The pale green petty spurge (*Euphorbia peplus*) is a common weed among vegetables and in flower beds. Growing from 10–30cm (4–12 in) in height it is an erect plant, usually with one to three stems near ground level but well-branched at the top, the stems repeatedly forking or dividing in threes. The tiny flowers are totally insignificant but are followed by three-lobed explosive capsules. More robust, and golden-green in colour with the upper branches in whorls, is sun spurge (*E. helioscopia*).

CONTROL Hoeing and hand pulling are the traditional ways of dealing with this weed. Most herbicides seem to be ineffective, but simazine and dichlobenil are effective.

Thistle, creeping Creeping thistle (*Cirsium arvense*) is one of the most pernicious of all perennial weeds. Its roots penetrate deeply and spread far. From them arise erect stems 60–120cm (2–4 ft) tall, bear-

Above: creeping thistle is one of the most persistent of weeds.

ing spiny leaves and lilac flower heads.
CONTROL Digging out as much of the root system as possible, followed by regular hoeing, will reduce this weed to manageable proportions but is seldom a permanent cure. Dichlobenil is the most efficient herbicide. MCPA or 2,4-D are successful if painted on the leaves.

Trefoil, *see* Clover.

Below: rosebay willowherb.

Twitch, *see* Grasses.

Willowherbs Rosebay willowherb (*Epilobium angustifolium*) is seldom a weed of gardens unless they are long-neglected. It produces thickets of wand-like stems clad with willow-shaped leaves and topped by spires of showy, rose-purple flowers. It spreads far and fast and every piece of root is capable of producing one or more shoots.

Several other clump-forming, less attractive willowherbs sometimes occur as weeds. They have smaller leaves and flowers, the latter paler in colour and sparingly carried on long, stalk-like embryo seed pods.
CONTROL Rosebay should be dug out as cleanly as possible, the re-growth being treated with dichlobenil. Where it can safely be used, sodium chlorate gives a good kill. The other willowherbs can easily be pulled out and are killed by paraquat/diquat or dichlobenil.

Winter heliotrope Winter heliotrope (*Petasites fragrans*) is a good example of a plant introduced for garden ornament which, in some areas at least, has become a nuisance. Winter-green, and with handsome, rounded, 15cm (6 in) wide, long-stalked leaves, in late winter and spring it bears spikes of heavily scented, mauve flower heads like those of a large groundsel. The creeping rhizomes soon form large colonies where the soil is fertile and there is shelter from cold winds.
CONTROL The large rhizomes are fairly near the surface and not difficult to dig out. Response to herbicides is largely unknown but glyphosate is worth trying.

Yarrow Also known as milfoil, common yarrow, (*Achillea millefolium*) is mainly a weed of neglected lawns. It stands mowing well and then appears as dark green, mossy patches composed of slender, deeply dissected leaves. If allowed to go uncut it grows 40–60cm (16–24 in) tall with flattened heads of white or pinkish flowers. 'Cerise Queen' is a cerise-red form grown in the flower border.
CONTROL All the approved lawn weed killers if regularly applied, keep this plant in check but seldom kill it outright. Small infestations are best cut out, and the holes re-turfed or seeded.

Yellow cress, creeping In moist soils, creeping yellow cress (*Rorippa sylvestris*) can be a real nuisance. It is a perennial with small pinnate leaves and creeping and sprawling stems 15–30cm (6–12 in) or so tall. Tiny, four-petalled, yellow flowers are carried in branched spikes. The slender roots are much branched and spread widely, emmitting shoots as they go.
CONTROL Curiously enough the response to herbicides of this plant is largely unknown. MCPA, 2,4-D, dichlobenil and glyphosate are all worth trying. Digging first and hoeing will weaken.

INDEX